SCALING SALES SUCCESS

SCALING SALES SUCCESS

16 Key Principles For Sales Leaders

David Mattson

President/CEO, Sandler Training

Jacket cover photo: Revelation

Hardcover: ISBN: 978-1-7351472-6-0

Ebook: ISBN: 978-1-7351472-2-2

To all the true sales leaders who commit to ongoing learning and development, both for their teams and for themselves.

CONTENTS

ACKNOWLEDGMENTS

MY DEEP GRATITUDE goes out to the many clients, strategic partners, and Sandler employees and franchisees who supported and encouraged me as I wrote this book. In particular, I'd like to thank Bill Bartlett for his vitally important contributions and his many insights. I must also thank Tom Ziglar, Sam Reese, Jonathan Farrington, Bob Perkins, Mike Philipps, and the many far-flung members of the Sandler team—Yusuf Toropov, Rachel Miller, Lori Ames, Shannon Haaf Howell, Margaret Stevens Jacks, Laura Matthews, Jerry Dorris, Elizabeth Faust, Jena Heffernan, Sarah Prokopchak, Denni Griffith, Tom Wilson, and Désirée Pilachowski—who made invaluable contributions to this project.

INTRODUCTION

THIS BOOK IS focused on sales leadership. I wrote it for people who are responsible for the performance of a sales team.

Leadership in sales is a very different skill from day-to-day management. This is because leadership is focused on the business, whereas management is devoted to solving problems that arise in the business. More of the "soft skills"—rapport-building, listening, public speaking, and so on—are required for effective leadership than are required for management.

That may seem to suggest that leadership is the easier of the two paths, but the truth is that leadership is far harder for many people because it is less tactical. Not all sales managers are sales leaders, but I believe all sales managers can learn to be sales leaders. In order to scale the success of your team in a way that supports ongoing, aggressive growth, leadership is a non-negotiable requirement. In fact, it is impossible to create scalable revenue growth, increasing it predictably and sustainably, with day-to-day management alone. For that kind of growth, you need real leadership, leadership that is committed to creating and supporting a special kind of sales team: the kind that corrects itself. This means engaging people.

In my experience, happy employees, and specifically happy salespeople, mean a happier—and healthier—business. If salespeople report to you, it is, I believe, your job as their leader to do what you can to make their experience working for you positive and enriching. Leadership, that quality most sought after in business, is best understood as the means by which you ensure that happiness.

When people are engaged and motivated and feel they are part of something larger than themselves—that is to say, when they are happy—they are more productive. This book aims to show you how to make that happen. It outlines the "rules of the road" for those leaders who are ready to make the journey necessary to transform a team of disengaged or marginally engaged salespeople into a cohesive, committed team capable of generating scalable revenue growth.

Study after study shows that companies that have strong leadership and higher levels of employee engagement tend to have lower employee turnover and better financial results than companies that don't. Most of the sales leaders we work with have seen this research. They know what the statistics say and what the trends are. They know the implications for their team's production. But they also know their sales team is not as engaged as it could be. Their question is a simple one: "What can I do to close the engagement gap on my team and make scalable growth a reality, not just a target?"

My hope is that some of the ideas in the book will help you begin to close that gap. In addition to drawing heavily on my own experience as I worked on this, I read paper after paper and considered insight after insight from researchers and academics. Some of what they had to say I agreed with, some I didn't. Frankly, some of the ideas came from people who aren't in the leadership space and did not understand it. Other ideas came from people who had spent a lot of time in the trenches and who spoke from experience. I learned something from every source I could find, but in the end I found that the best advice came from the people who had put in time in the trenches by leading a sales team.

The point on which everyone with direct personal experience seems to agree is that all the important things individuals strive for—goal achievement, mission orientation, the sense of having made a contribution, the sense of having approached or attained one's full potential—depend upon the quality of the leadership present. You're not going to have an awesome culture in the team, for instance, if the decisions from the leader that directly affect the team's working culture are not driven by integrity.

A University of Warwick study concluded that happy people were, on average, 12% more productive than others, with some performing as high as 20% above the control group.[1]

One vitally important goal is keeping your salespeople engaged—yet keeping employees engaged is not easy. If it were, everyone would do it. A major obstacle is that everything, and I do mean everything, flows downhill. Your people are always watching what you do and listening to what you say (and don't say). Some look to you for inspiration, some want to mimic what you do with their teams, and others are especially tuned in to inconsistencies in your messaging and your actions. Not only that, the environment in which your team operates is constantly changing, sometimes at astonishing speed. The rapid pace of change can be confusing and disorienting. If it is confusing and disorienting to you, it is going to be confusing and disorienting to your salespeople.

All of this makes it extremely difficult to engage salespeople and keep them engaged. Given these circumstances, I believe it is vitally important for anyone who finds themselves in a sales leadership position to commit to being the best they can possibly be and to create and follow a plan of continuous growth and personal/professional development. With that commitment in mind, I would submit that learning to master the sixteen rules listed below needs to be part of the development plan for any and every leader. Think of them as operating principles.

1. **Lead with Integrity.** Know what you stand for—and communicate accordingly.
2. **Don't Get Emotionally Involved.** Disengage from the drama.
3. **Check Your Own Pipeline First.** Keep an eye out for talent; avoid the most common onboarding mistakes.
4. **Model and Coach Excellence with Private Meetings.** Use one-on-one discussions to support growth and development.
5. **Tap Into the *Why*.** Find out what drives people on a personal level.
6. **Begin with Their Point of View.** Understand and respect behavioral style and perspective.
7. **Be Strategically Inquisitive.** Ask questions that clarify all the important issues.

8. **Respect Their Truth.** Accept that yours is not the only point of view and that people are just as passionate about their opinion.
9. **Build Tomorrow's Leaders.** Set people up for success.
10. **Make Accountability the Norm.** Create a culture of accountability.
11. **Create Team Ownership of Ideas and Solutions.** Leverage the wisdom and creativity of the team; give others the credit.
12. **Don't Wimp Out.** Set priorities that push you beyond your comfort zone.
13. **Develop the Right Processes and the Tools That Support Them.** Create and implement playbooks.
14. **Macromanage.** Let people do their jobs.
15. **Become a Learning Team.** Commit to personal and professional development.
16. **Be Ready for Anything.** Plan, prepare, and then be flexible.

These are the building blocks of effective leadership, which is what makes scalable revenue growth possible. Learning to grasp and follow these rules takes practice, but if you commit to making them part of who you are when you show up for work each morning, then you have what it takes to be a true sales leader, not just a sales manager. Even someone who has struggled with their own development as a leader in the past can make rapid progress by focusing consistently on these sixteen core principles.

ARE GREAT LEADERS MADE OR BORN?

Many people imagine that good leaders are simply "born that way"—that someone either has or doesn't have the DNA that supports certain distinctive traits and predispositions. Supposedly, these inborn traits and predispositions add up to that elusive quality popularly known as "leadership potential." That's not our experience here at Sandler. Great leadership can be learned. While there's no substitute for being passionate about what you are doing, there are also principles that can be learned and mastered to increase your leadership effectiveness.

After more than five decades of working with sales leaders across all industries and sectors, we at Sandler have found that developing leadership is a matter of sustained effort and focus on the sixteen critical principles you just read. The words of the principles can't replace experience, of course, but do we see them as necessary starting points that lead aspiring sales leaders toward the necessary experience. It would be nice if every new sales leader could skip all the mistakes and still get the benefit of all the lessons learned, but that is not how mastery is developed—it is developed through gradual learning.

The pattern of gradual learning, of course, does not play out only in the business world, but in all walks of life. People grow, change, and adapt over time. Some of them develop what look like "natural" leadership skills, but these are really the accumulation of hard work and experience. For example, few of the people who knew him in the 1920s considered Harry Truman a natural-born leader. He had dropped out of college, started a business that went bankrupt, and went down to electoral defeat for a county judge position. A 2017 poll of historians, however, identified him as one of the greatest presidents in U.S. history.

Great leaders, in other words, are made, not born. This is as true of sales leaders as it is of any other kind of leader. They can be naturally outgoing, or naturally reserved—naturally task-focused, or naturally people-focused. None of that has anything to do with whether a person can develop sales leadership skills and learn to adapt their communications and their strengths to the individual and the situation at hand.

As a sales leader, you can always improve. In seeking out your own optimum level of performance, though, remember that you have been shaped by what you observe and how you were treated by your own leaders and other important people in your life.

You may find yourself perpetuating bad leadership habits you saw firsthand only because you didn't know better at the time.

Perhaps you've seen the Progressive Insurance commercials featuring a "Dr. Rick," who intones solemnly, "My job is to help new homeowners who have turned into their parents." It's hilarious—but that commercial also serves as a reminder that people often really do mimic their parents, usually without realizing it. I often catch myself in the act, saying to myself, "I sound just like Dad," or "That's what Mom would do." You may have had a similar experience. Here's the point: In your professional life, you are just as likely to unconsciously mimic the people to whom you reported earlier in your career. It's your responsibility to understand those influences and to break the mold when necessary.

My daughter came home one day and told us that she wanted to be a nurse. She had given this a lot of thought. My wife and I supported her in that decision because it obviously meant a lot to her. It wasn't my place to tell her to follow in my footsteps instead of doing what she wanted to do, which was to serve people in a healthcare setting. Isn't that the best way to respond to a child's interests? To encourage them to grow and develop over time in a way that makes sense to them? Of course it is.

The key phrase in any such discussion is, as David Sandler knew, "encourage people to grow and develop."

He didn't believe, and I don't believe, that there is any such thing as a born salesperson—or, for that matter, a born sales leader. Are pilots born? Are doctors born? Are landscapers born? Are baseball players born? Of course, the answer is no. It takes years of hard work to get to the point where you can make a contribution in any of those areas, much less excel in one of them. Sales leadership is the same. If you have chosen this as your path and you want to make a personal commitment to get better at it over time, I wrote this book for you.

A side note: In sharing these foundational leadership principles with sales leaders, we found that people got great results from following them, not only on the job but in their other roles in life. Many of the rules in this book have universal relevance to anyone and everyone taking on personal responsibility for a team's performance. However, my first and most important priority in assembling these sixteen rules has been to help sales leaders master the leadership skills that enable them and their teams to post dramatic, scalable, and sustainable increases in revenue over an extended period. These sixteen operating principles work in developing effective sales leaders in any industry.

Excellence in sales leadership is, I believe, a lifelong journey, not a destination. The rules you will be learning in these pages—most of which I learned first from my own mentor David Sandler, the founder of our company—are signposts that can guide you and keep you on the right course as you make that journey.

RULE 1

Lead with Integrity

KNOW WHAT YOU STAND FOR—AND COMMUNICATE ACCORDINGLY.

"Be more concerned with your character than your reputation, because your character is what you really are, while your reputation is merely what others think you are."

—John Wooden

A WHILE BACK, one of my UK contacts, the managing director (equivalent of a CEO) at a major client company, told me a fascinating story—one that illustrates the immense power of setting the right personal example, which is really what this first rule, "Lead with Integrity," is all about.

The managing director noticed that there was limited parking space in the company headquarters garage. People were complaining about the shortage and putting up traffic cones in an attempt to save choice spots. It wasn't pretty. The ongoing arguments meant there was always stress first thing every morning, not just for the managing director but for the whole organization. One day he asked himself a question: *Why not ride my bike to the office?* He didn't live that far from the building; biking was good exercise; and, by biking in, he'd himself avoid the stress of trying to find a parking spot. There was never any difficulty finding a place in the garage to put a bike.

So he started biking to work. People noticed. Then, the most amazing thing happened. Without him having said a word or issuing any kind of instructions or suggestions about how to get to work, people changed their behaviors. Within six months, the building's garage was full of bicycles.

This is a true story, one worth studying closely, about the power of personal leadership. Here's the key takeaway: Whether they're consciously aware of it or not, people model their behavior and their decision paths on those of their leaders. It is always the leaders who set the standard. This simple, inescapable fact means that sales leaders carry a certain moral responsibility with every choice they make and every action they take. The question is, are they setting the right example?

As a leader, you constantly need to ask yourself:

> "Would I want everyone on the team approaching their decisions in the way I am approaching this decision?"

"Would I want everyone on the team taking this course of action, if they were faced with a situation similar to the one I am facing?"

"Do I want people to act the way I am acting right now?"

"Do I want people communicating the way I am communicating right now?"

At the end of the day, these questions point toward a single, vitally important word: *integrity*. Now, if you go to the dictionary, you'll find that this word features two complementary, overlapping meanings. The first meaning of integrity is "the quality of being honest and having strong moral principles." The second meaning is "the state of being whole and undivided." I mention this because both of those definitions are required to grasp what this first, and perhaps most important, leadership rule is all about.

Great sales leaders have strong moral principles that are not layered on or factored in as some kind of afterthought. Their principles are essential, non-negotiable elements of who they are as human beings. Are they perfect people? No. But they know that if they deviate from what they know is right, that always leaves a gap, a deficit, a lack of wholeness—something that must be repaired.

Just as you can't drive a car with one of the wheels missing, you won't get very far as a sales leader without integrity. Eventually there is going to be a breakdown because the rest of the team is going to be following your example whether you mean for them to or not. Any lack of integrity on your part is going to echo and multiply. If your aim is to build a team that delivers the kind of success that is both measurable and scalable, you always need to start from a place of integrity. Understand that people watch what you do, they see how you make decisions and interact with others, and then they adjust their behavior and their thinking to match up with yours.

There are three big areas where you can make leading with integrity the starting point for yourself and your team. Let's look at each of them now.

SALES LEADERSHIP KEY 1: KNOW WHAT YOU STAND FOR.

What are your values? What are the principles from which you draw strength, the core commitments that you are not willing to compromise? What are the values that guide you, your team, and your organization, as you answer the question, "How do we do things around here?"

You may remember the film *Gladiator*, starring Russell Crowe as the Roman general Maximus. Before going into battle, Maximus reminds himself and others of his values by saying the following words out loud: "Strength and honor." Drawing on that strength and upholding that honor is not always easy—in fact, it is sometimes excruciatingly difficult for Maximus—but these values are what define him as a person and the movement he eventually leads.

Leaders need a similar set of words they can appeal to as their moral compass, both for themselves and their organization. For instance: "Mutual respect, clarity, professionalism, and transparency." I'm not saying you must make these specific words your personal or team values—but I am saying that you need to identify some set of words that briefly express who you are and what you stand for, even when the pressure is on.

People need to see you defending your own values, even when it would be easier not to. For instance, if you say you value respect and professionalism but you keep someone on your sales team who consistently abuses those values because they are bringing in money, that's a failure of leadership. Your people need to see you making the tough decisions that support your values. They need to know what to expect. They will respect you and work harder to support your vision when they see you making difficult decisions that are consistent with what you truly believe.

SALES LEADERSHIP KEY 2: BUILD TRUST. BE CONSISTENT AND CONGRUENT.

Creating and expanding trust is a matter of consistency and congruence.

Let's look at consistency first. People want to trust you, but to do so they need to see evidence that you aren't making decisions in a haphazard or random way. They want to be able to count on you. This means settling on a predictable schedule for interacting with them and then using a clear, comprehensible set of standards for making decisions that affect them so that they're not taken by surprise.

One classic way to destroy trust is to try to please everyone on your team, a habit that always leads to inconsistent decision making. Leaders who try to please everyone end up pleasing no one. When your standards constantly shift to keep people happy, they can't tell which way the wind is going to blow on any given day. There's no consistent, objective standard guiding the decisions. Being popular is nice, but it is not always possible.

Let's look next at congruence. This means making sure your words match up with your deeds and beliefs. It also means doing what you say you are going to do. Is your word your bond? If the people who report to you all agree that it is, then you don't have a problem with congruence. If they have to stop and think about a trail of broken commitments, then you have some work to do on this score.

Think of a specific public figure you personally find hard to trust. Have you got someone in mind? Great. Now, why don't you trust that person? I'm willing to bet it's because their messaging doesn't come across as sincere to you. Maybe they made commitments they didn't follow through on, and they hoped no one would notice. Maybe there were times when that person was not willing to say, "I don't know." Maybe the person said things they thought sounded good on the surface, but simply didn't align with reality. That's all incongruence. It makes people doubt what the leader has to say, even when it's true.

When you are incongruent, people come away from discussions with you wondering whether you're saying what you really believe. They waste a lot of time and energy trying to figure out if you have given them the full picture. The only way you can build trust as a leader is to make your thinking, behavior, and decisions line up. That means leveling with people, even if that entails sharing a point of view or a decision they disagree with. If you are following the same values all the time in making big decisions, you will usually find that it is easier for people to understand why a given decision didn't go their way.

If the only truth you have to share at the moment is, "I can't talk about that yet," or "I'm still working on that," go ahead and say that. People don't always want to hear those answers, but if they are all you've got to share, share them. Be very careful not to confuse a desire to tell the truth with a desire for acceptance. The person on the other side of the conversation may not agree or like what you are saying. That is a separate topic. If you avoid the conversation or shade the message in an effort to avoid confrontation, that will only cause more issues to deal with down the line. When you make choices that undercut the truth and erode trust, you will have to pay for those choices at some point—and so will your team.

The moral here is pretty simple. Shoot straight with people if you want them to trust you. Be consistent, and tell them the truth.

According to Trust Across America, the stock share price of the ten most trustworthy public companies in the United States (using that organization's methodology for establishing trustworthiness) have outperformed the S&P 500 by over 25% since 2010.[2]

SALES LEADERSHIP KEY 3: WHEN YOU MAKE A MISTAKE, OWN IT.

A big part of integrity is taking personal responsibility for your actions and decisions as a leader. Other people may decide to play the CYA ("cover your anatomy") game. As a leader, you can't.

You're not going to make the right decision 100% of the time. But you also know that, if you're following the right process and the right methodology, if you're thinking about all the things you should be thinking about, then a bad decision is always going to be a learning experience. Accept that, take responsibility for what happened, and move on.

Blaming others is a waste of precious time and energy. If you are tempted to blame a member of the sales team for a problem, any problem, rather than assume personal responsibility for the team's performance, then you are outside of integrity. Many people don't get this, but it's an essential element of the leader's job description that you cannot overlook. You don't get to point fingers. You are the one making the call about what to do and how to do it.

When something goes wrong, just own up to it, be straight with the team about what happened, and fix the problem. (See also Rule 10's Sales Leadership Key, "Hold yourself accountable first." We will look at its implications for the team in more depth in that chapter.) Show people, by your own example, what owning a mistake looks like. Learn from it so you don't have to repeat it, then keep going. Isn't that what you want your team to do when they make a mistake?

SALES LEADERSHIP KEYS: RULE 1

1. Know what you stand for.
2. Build trust. Be consistent and congruent.
3. When you make a mistake, own it.

RULE 2

Don't Get Emotionally Involved

DISENGAGE FROM THE DRAMA.

"Pastimes and games are substitutes for the real living of real intimacy."

—ERIC BERNE, in *Games People Play: The Psychology of Human Relationships*

REMEMBER THE MANY old Peanuts comic strips where Lucy holds the football for Charlie Brown to kick, and then pulls it away at the last moment so that he goes flying? That was drama, and drama is not limited to the comic strips. Daytime soap operas and reality shows are some of the most enduringly popular things on TV, and they are each built around the same principle of creating drama. People are entertained by the chaos, which is why they have been tuning in to these shows by the millions for decades now.

Guess what? Drama shows up in the workplace all the time,

although it's not always so entertaining. This second rule is all about how to minimize or even eliminate the drama in your team.

Drama is just another word for dysfunction—something that doesn't work. When we at Sandler talk about not getting emotionally involved in workplace drama, we're not talking about turning yourself into an uncaring robot. We're talking about the ability to disengage from games that don't go anywhere, don't get anything accomplished, and waste precious time, energy, and goodwill.

Sometimes employee drama is based on a simple (but dysfunctional) desire to stir things up. One study, conducted by researcher Christine Porath, concluded that 4% of people who engage in incivility in the workplace do so simply because they "believe it's fun and think they can get away with it."[3]

It is all too easy to get involved in drama, as a participant or as an observer. However, saying no to drama is a requirement for effective sales leadership. Choosing not to fake people out by putting down a football you don't intend to hold steady is essential—and so is declining to rush toward the ball when you know it is going to be pulled away at the last moment. Disengaging from dysfunctional games is a predictable trait of high-performing leaders. It's a great principle to follow at work—and everywhere else, for that matter.

In our one-on-one coaching sessions or during group events, when we ask sales leaders whether they agree that workplace drama is counterproductive, they always nod their heads in agreement. Who wants more drama? But here's the challenge. People often create drama without even realizing it. In fact, all too often it is the leader who is the prime instigator of toxic drama in the workplace.

Have you ever been on the receiving end of that kind of drama? Have you ever listened as a manager decided to throw everything on the table during a sales team meeting—the good, the bad, and the ugly? How did you feel when your boss started talking about specific people who hadn't handled a prospect interaction properly? How did you feel when the boss was talking about you? Was it awkward? Demotivating? Even humiliating?

Sure, your boss might have prefaced this discussion by saying something like, "Let's just save some time and say this once so everyone can hear the message and act on it." But that didn't change what was happening. You were getting called out in front of your peers—and it was weird. That weirdness was drama. That finger-pointing event caused drama, which was nothing but a waste of time.

When you as a sales leader have an issue with the way a

salesperson is doing the job (or not doing the job), how do you raise that issue? We recommend doing this in private, as part of a confidential discussion that is designed to help the employee grow and develop professionally. Having the conversation in public backfires almost every time because it puts people on the spot, even if you feel that what you have to say has been couched as constructive feedback.

Most sales leaders we work with in our coaching have to take a deep breath and do a little self-assessment at this point. Perhaps you're in the same situation right now. As you stop to consider the consequences of making the employee uncomfortable in front of others, you may also want to consider this next question: Does what you actually say to salespeople about a challenge that you are trying to address ever sound like any of the conversational openings you see below?

"Lee, why didn't you do X?" (In which X is what you would have done.)

"Lee, what were you thinking? You know better than that. I expected more of you."

"Lee, how many times have I told you to do Y?" (In which Y is a part of a process that you and Lee have discussed before.)

"Lee, I've had it. I'm sick and tired of you letting me down. I warned you about Z, and now that it's happened, you've made me look like an idiot to the whole company. You're going to have to step up and fix this—not me. I don't want to hear about Z happening again." (In which Z is a negative outcome you had hoped to avoid.)

If even one of those sentences rings the tiniest, faintest bell, there is likely an issue with drama that you may be initiating with your salespeople—which means that your relationship with your salespeople is not what it could be. And, neither is their performance level.

Each of those very common approaches to highlighting a problem represents a football being snatched away from Charlie Brown. When you start an exchange like that, you are setting the salesperson up for failure. Drama does not help people grow and develop.

Recognizing that simple fact is usually not enough—disengaging from the drama habit doesn't happen automatically. It takes effort and practice over time. There are three critical skill sets that support the goal of limiting emotional involvement in workplace games. I'll give you a brief overview of all three of them now.

SALES LEADERSHIP KEY 4: LEARN TO SPOT YOUR CRITICAL PARENT AND YOUR CHILD.

In the first three conversational openings I just shared with you, the manager is communicating from what the psychoanalytic theory known as transactional analysis (TA) would call the Critical Parent ego state. Let me take a moment to explain.

David Sandler, the best boss I ever had, used TA as his human-relations model to back up his reasoning for why buyers and sellers—and, just as important, salespeople and managers—act the way they do. TA assumes that humans operate out of three ego states.

- The Parent ego state contains unedited recordings of what you saw and heard your parents or other authority figures do and say during your first five years of life.
  - Sometimes, parental messages were critical, judgmental, or prejudicial. They were the do's and don'ts you heard growing up. For example, "Don't talk back!" These are called Critical Parent messages.
  - Sometimes the messages were more nurturing: "Everybody makes mistakes." These are Nurturing Parent messages.
- The Child ego state is where many decisions originate—not

just decisions about how to fulfill a given task at work, but all kinds of decisions. The Child is that little six-year-old inside who, feeling a particular impulse or wave of emotion at a moment's notice, says, "I want this," and "I want to do that." Or, just as likely: "I don't want this," and "I don't want to do that."

- The Adult ego state acts much like a computer, processing data supplied by the other two ego states, as well as data it collects. The Adult is logical, rational, and analytical. The Adult solves problems and reckons probability. Think of Data in *Star Trek: The Next Generation* (or Mr. Spock if you're an original series fan) and you've got a pretty good idea of what the Adult ego state is.

Here is the point. Most sales managers go into massive Critical Parent mode when they realize a salesperson has made a mistake. They say things like, "You need to straighten up and fly right," and they think it's going to work. The truth is it never works, although the salesperson sometimes produces good results in spite of what the manager says.

A simple rule of thumb you can use to evaluate your own communications is this one: Any time you criticize someone or tell someone directly what they should or shouldn't do, you are communicating from your Critical Parent ego state.

Why not take a close look at the first three conversational openings with Lee that I shared with you earlier? You may notice that each of them begins with a criticism, a direct or indirect command, or a combination of the two. Critical Parent messaging is totally counterproductive when it comes to motivating salespeople to change their behavior—and it's particularly ineffective when it's delivered in public, as a put-down. All it causes is emotional pain and the desire to make that pain stop. In such situations, salespeople don't focus on the content of what you are saying so much as they focus on how what you say makes them feel. They then internalize that feeling. Most of the time, they don't ask for clarification, and they make the issue much worse in their mind than it actually is.

What about that fourth response I shared with you, the one where the manager tells Lee, "I've had it!" and improvises from there? That's coming from the Child ego state. Here's the tipoff: The focus is on what the manager doesn't want to experience again, isn't going to put up with, and so on. Communications from the Child ego state are driven by emotion and by what people want or don't want. Exchanges that begin from the Child can be even more toxic and debilitating than communications originating from the Critical Parent for the simple reason that the salesperson is very likely to respond in kind, at which point the discussion consists of dueling six-year-olds. That's not a great place from which to identify, diagnose, or resolve a performance challenge.

It's important to learn to recognize and step away from communication that originates from the Critical Parent or the Child ego state so that you can communicate from the Nurturing Parent or the Adult ego state instead. This is what I mean by not getting emotionally involved.

Pulling this off means overcoming ingrained habits of communicating from the Critical Parent and the Child ego state. It means patiently putting TA into practice as your personal leadership productivity tool. This practice is worth getting personal coaching support for, because TA works. It helps you learn to use your Nurturing Parent and Adult ego states as default settings when it comes to contact with salespeople—and everyone else. This leads to much better outcomes.

Here's an example of what a private, TA-driven discussion with Lee might sound like. Note that it incorporates a mutual agreement about the agenda and "ground rules" for the discussion, an agreement we at Sandler call an Up-Front Contract.

"Lee, thanks for the time today. I know we're together to talk about the Ideas, Inc. account. Are we still good for that today?" (Lee agrees.)

"Great. Let's do this. Give me an overview of where we are and anything you feel I should know. Please let me know along the way where you feel the roadblocks are, any questions you may have, or any areas where you need help. OK? That will help me get up to speed. I will be asking questions along the way and sharing some thoughts on what we should do to overcome the roadblocks. Fair?" (Lee agrees.)

"We've set aside thirty minutes. I just want to make sure we leave some time at the end—maybe 10 minutes—to summarize what we decided and the next steps. Is that all right?" (Lee agrees.)

"OK. Is there anything you would like to add to the agenda?" (Lee shares any issues/agenda items.)

It is worth emphasizing that this is a private coaching conversation. A safe, one-on-one meeting is the only appropriate place to share constructive feedback with an employee. We'll look more closely at the specifics of how to share that feedback in Rule 4.

A conversation that opens this way sets the other person up for success, generates much better information and next steps, and allows the leader to serve as a positive example for the salesperson and for the team. The most effective sales leaders look for ways to co-create solutions with salespeople—by operating exclusively from the Nurturing Parent and Adult ego states. They stay away from the Critical Parent and the Child.

It takes some practice—it is easy to forget how important not getting emotionally involved is in the heat of the moment. Here are some brief tips that will help you remember and get back on track quickly—and keep the discussion on the Adult-to-Adult level.

- Give strokes. (Strokes are validation that the other person will recognize as authentic.) That's the Nurturing Parent.
- Stick to the facts. That's the Adult.
- If you're ever tempted to criticize or issue commands or to talk about what you personally do or don't want, look for a way to ask a constructive question instead. Leave the Critical Parent and the Child out of the discussion.

SALES LEADERSHIP KEY 5: FOCUS ON THE ROLE, NOT THE IDENTITY.

Any meaningful discussion about keeping communication at the Adult-to-Adult level has to incorporate the concept of self-worth. The Sandler concept of self-worth, or Identity/Role Theory, is based on the separation of identity (who you are) from role (what you do).

This distinction is critical. Role performance is based on the behaviors you perform in order to be successful in your job. Identity is something very different. Identity is who you are. Who you are is not determined by how you perform within a given role. Your sense of self-worth, as described by David Sandler, is derived from the complex blending of who you are (your identity) and what you do (your role).

Your identity as a person always rates 10 on a scale of 10. What does that mean, exactly? It means that, as a human being, you are perfect and worth as much—right now, just as you are—as every other human being. Your rating within a role, however, at any given moment, may come in at something less than 10—that's not unusual. Are you a perfect golfer? A perfect leader? A perfect spouse? Maybe not. But you are a 10 out of 10 as a person, and that must be taken into account when it comes to your own sense of self-worth.

This dynamic holds true, not just for you, but for every salesperson who reports to you.

It's vitally important, when communicating with members of the sales team, not to confuse identity and role. If you focus too much on the role (which is what usually happens)—if how people perform within that role is all that is ever discussed or acknowledged by you—you will miss the critical fact that people can only perform in their role to the degree that they believe in themselves.

Successful leaders understand the importance of a strong identity. They know that a strong identity helps a person make the difficult changes necessary for improved performance. They look for ways to reinforce a team member's belief in themselves as a person. The leader's own secure sense of self-worth can serve as a subtle, but motivating, role model in this regard.

SALES LEADERSHIP KEY 6: STAY OUT OF THE DRAMA TRIANGLE.

As I have already mentioned, drama is one of those things that brings in great TV ratings and lots of views on social media. The massive popularity of soap operas and reality-show programs proves this. People can't help watching conflict, and they're particularly interested in watching toxic conflict. Human beings love watching drama. But as a sales leader, you don't want drama in the workplace. There, drama is poison.

Your personal life may be filled with drama, but you need to make sure your professional life is drama free. How do you do that? One great way to pull it off is to study something called the Karpman Drama Triangle. This tool, developed by Dr. Stephen Karpman, helps you identify destructive interactions that can take place in conflict situations. At its most basic level, the Drama Triangle helps you identify and avoid toxic games that people play. Once you know what's happening, you can stay out of the drama and come up with a better approach. The only way to win the Drama Triangle game is not to play.

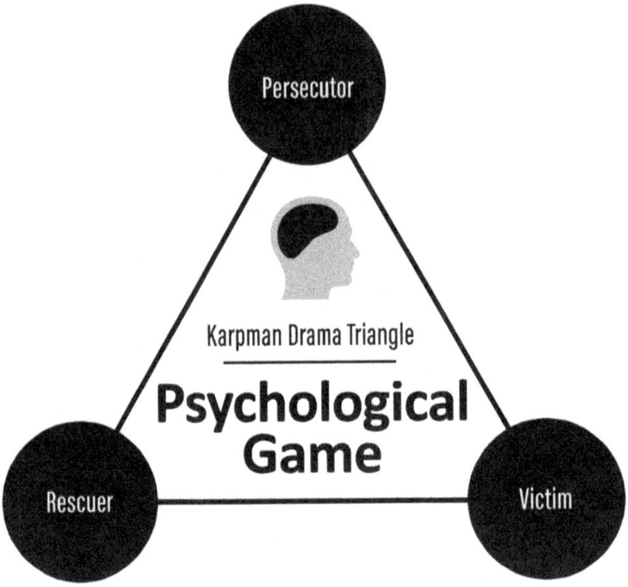

There are three positions on the triangle: a persecutor, a victim, and a rescuer. The rules are simple—when you or anyone else takes on any one of these roles, there is drama. Each person can only play one role at a time, but the roles can flip around very quickly. A person can start out as a victim, for instance, and quickly move into a situation where they are the persecutor.

Consider that "I've had it" messaging the manager loaded on Lee. Here it is again:

"Lee, I've had it. I'm sick and tired of you letting me down.

I warned you about Z, and now that it's happened, you've made me look like an idiot to the whole company. You're going to have to step up and fix this—not me. I don't want to hear about Z happening again."

Remember that this emotional messaging is coming from the sales manager's Child ego state. But look what else it is doing: It is painting a picture in which the manager's agency, the manager's personal involvement in creating a solution, is zero, because the employee has "let the manager down." The manager is the victim. That's not a grownup conversation. It's a conversation rooted in drama.

Suppose Lee responds by saying that the sales manager actually let Lee down, and offers all kinds of persuasive proof, including a long list of administrative mistakes and an even longer list of personal problems that the manager has insensitively refused to even ask about. Now there's a disagreement about who's the victim. Very often, when that happens, the manager will shift into persecutor mode: "Why in the world is it my job to fix the problems in your personal life?" Once those harsh words slip out, there are hurt feelings. A line has been crossed.

Kids know when they're in trouble, and so do grownups. In this case, the manager is likely to conclude that things have gotten out of hand, so they may try to repair the problem "just this once" by swooping in and fixing the whole Z situation themselves. Now they're the rescuer—and the cycle is complete. Not only that, it will repeat itself in a week, in a day, or in a couple of hours.

Do you see how it works? You get out of one spot on the triangle by moving to another spot, but nothing constructive happens. If you don't recognize the cycle and learn to step away from it, the drama will never go away. Your job as leader is to identify the drama and stop it. That means having Adult-to-Adult conversations and co-creating solutions to problems.

SALES LEADERSHIP KEYS: RULE 2

4. Learn to spot your Critical Parent and your Child.
5. Focus on the role, not the identity.
6. Stay out of the Drama Triangle.

RULE 3

Check Your Own Pipeline First

KEEP AN EYE OUT FOR TALENT; AVOID THE MOST COMMON ONBOARDING MISTAKES.

"An employee's job is to give his or her best work every day. A manager's job is to give the employee a good reason to come back to work tomorrow."

—Liz Ryan, CEO and founder of Human Workplace

MANY SALES LEADERS are used to inquiring about the health of a salesperson's pipeline, also known as a sales funnel, as it's the lifeblood of selling success. Leaders want to know: How many viable leads need to be fed consistently into the top of that funnel in order for this salesperson to meet the agreed-upon income target? Where are those leads coming from? What qualification process will determine which leads actually connect to business problems the company can solve, budgets available to solve them, and decision makers who are ready to discuss the possibility of working together?

These are all vitally important questions, and of course they need to be asked. But even before you check in on the health of the pipeline of those who report to you, be sure to accept that you, also, have a pipeline—one that is all too often both neglected and unhealthy. Just as the salespeople who report to you have a professional obligation to keep their sales pipeline filled with opportunities, you have a professional obligation to keep your talent pipeline filled with prospective employees who will continually raise the performance bar. For a salesperson, it's revenue production that determines effectiveness. For a sales leader, it's superior talent acquisition.

In fact, your pipeline's health actually matters more than the salesperson's does, for the simple reason that your pipeline affects multiple income streams and has a bigger impact on the growth trajectory of your organization. Talent pipeline health is one of the critical indicators that shows how well you are doing your job. It's part of our coaching to advise senior leadership to track the specific behaviors that support recruiting and onboarding success—such as initial calls with prospective hires who are referred by current hires. We urge top leadership to make these metrics part of each sales leader's behavioral plan and part of the performance evaluation.

Just as a salesperson has a responsibility to prospect consistently for new revenue opportunities and move those opportunities through the pipeline, sales leaders have a responsibility to prospect consistently for new talent and to move that talent through the recruitment and development phases of their pipeline.

Let's look at each of those phases now.

SALES LEADERSHIP KEY 7: MANAGE THE RECRUITMENT PHASE OF YOUR PIPELINE STRATEGICALLY.

First things first: Accept that recruitment of salespeople is a long game, and, ultimately, it's the sales leader's job—not HR's. The people in human resources may have lots to offer, but they aren't as close to the action as you are, they don't have as much direct experience as you do, and they don't have as much of a stake in the success or failure of the hire as you do. So start by acknowledging your own responsibility to network and keep an eye out for talented people.

After all, you are the one personally responsible for the heavy costs associated with a bad sales hire—which, just in case you were wondering, are reliably estimated at between ten and twenty times a salesperson's base salary. That's a big number, one that is worth considering closely. You've probably heard the old saying: "If you think hiring a professional is expensive, try hiring an amateur." That warning is doubly true when it comes to salespeople. It's also a potent reminder that each and every sales hire is a big decision with big consequences. Identifying talent for your team is your job, no one else's. Hiring is an ongoing, essential part of your job, no matter how frequently or rarely it happens. Bringing on a new salesperson is a decision that you must always make by design, not by default.

In many organizations, unfortunately, the hiring decision is made by default. Managers don't recruit and expand their contact networks until there is an opening to fill. Often initial screening and interviewing is offloaded to others. Or, it may swing to the other extreme, with leaders getting no input from anyone else on the team and making hiring decisions impulsively, following that elusive, indefinable standard, "I know talent when I see it." If sales leaders do not prospect for new talent consistently—in exactly the way they expect sales representatives to prospect for new clients consistently—they are caught off guard when a salesperson quits. They then have to scramble to hire a replacement, which is a recipe for bad decisions. The very worst sales hires are made if leaders only recruit when the smoke detector goes off.

The best sales hires, on the other hand, are made when you "arm" yourself with what I call an "always recruiting mentality." ARM means that you constantly reach out to prospective sales hires, constantly cultivate new relationships, and constantly evaluate talent. This doesn't mean you are making job offers all the time (unless that is part of a strategic plan), but it does mean that you become proficient at being a talent scout, always on the lookout for those who can bring the team to the next level.

Just as important, ARM also means that you have and are familiar with a comprehensive, clear, written job description, one based on a carefully considered success profile for each sales position you are likely to be hiring for. ARM means you are prepared to evaluate each candidate you talk to, formally or informally, against this success profile. A great tool for evaluating potential team members is what we at Sandler call the SEARCH model.

SEARCH stands for skills, experience, attitude, results, cognitive skills, and habits. Set aside a few minutes to explore the questions below, and you will be well on your way to creating the success profile for any position on your team.*

- **Skills:** What are the specific skills needed to be a top performer in this position? Note that the skills necessary to keep an account are not all the same skills necessary to acquire an account in the first place. By the same token, if your goal is to recapture an account, there will be a certain

* Of course, the six elements of the SEARCH model can be easily adapted to any role that you hope to fill, not just to sales positions.

combination of skills that supports that goal. If your goal is to expand an existing account, that will demand yet another combination of skills. Although there is some overlap in the skill sets required for success in each of these areas, the lists of required skills are not going to be identical. So, which of these four objectives do you expect the salesperson to spend most of their time pursuing? Based on that, what are the relevant skill sets you should be looking for? What is the most important skill set? Someone who is looking to acquire Fortune 1000 accounts, for instance, should have a proven ability to reach and begin business conversations with C-level decision makers.

- **Experience:** What level of experience does this sales job require? Note that experience within a given industry may not be as relevant as experience with a certain kind of selling. Someone with five years of experience in inbound sales in a given vertical may not thrive in the same vertical if they are responsible for initiating contact.
- **Attitude:** What mental attitudes are essential for success in this sales position? An abundance (as opposed to scarcity) mindset and a "we-first" (as opposed to "me-first") approach to business relationships are two obvious attitudinal traits you will want to look for. You will also want

someone with the capacity to bounce back from failure, stay focused on goals, remain positive in the face of adversity, and sustain a healthy self-concept. What verifiable experiences in the person's background demonstrate this kind of outlook? Last but certainly not least, you will want to ask yourself: Is this person not only able to do this job, but truly willing to do it?

- **Results:** What are the specific metrics a new hire will be accepting responsibility for delivering in this position? In other words, what are the measurable indicators of success? Consider both the lagging indicators (like closed sales) and the leading indicators that make the lagging indicators possible (like initial discussions with new prospects). What numerical outcomes will you be looking for? What timelines will connect to those outcomes?
- **Cognitive skills:** What kinds of cognitive skills—memory, logic, reasoning—are necessary for success in this sales position? What sorts of problems should this person be able to solve? What planning responsibilities do you expect this person to have? Take some time to answer these questions in detail. Saying that you expect to hire someone who can "hit the ground running" is not an ideal answer.

- **Habits:** What are the work habits that the top performers in this sales position exhibit right now? For instance, do all of your top performers make a habit of conducting quarterly business reviews with major clients? What else do these top performers do routinely and with a high degree of proficiency to deliver success within the role?

As the sales leader, it is your responsibility not only to know the answers to these questions but also to use your business and personal networks to identify a steady stream of prospective hires who seem likely to match the profile, even if you are not hiring right now. These are your hiring prospects. You also want to be proficient at disqualifying those who do not to hit all six requirements.

Let me emphasize: Even when you are not hiring (which may be most of the time) you should be prospecting. Just as the members of your sales team must have a viable base of potential buyers, you must have a viable base of potential hires so that you are ready to interview the right person when an opening does arise.

Hiring while you're in panic mode means you stress yourself (and others) out needlessly. Often, you might end up with low performers who do not meet the criteria for success within the role. Constantly managing the turnover of low performers who do not meet your success profile means you are forced to constantly raise the performance bar for the remainder of your team, and that does not make for high team morale. Instead, use SEARCH to make each new hire a positive addition to the team from the get-go.

SALES LEADERSHIP KEY 8: AVOID THE MOST COMMON ONBOARDING MISTAKES.

The comparison of the sales leader's pipeline to the salesperson's pipeline is still important as you consider what needs to happen after you identify someone who could be a good addition to the team. Think about it. A salesperson who gets a deal to the point of a verbal commitment but who doesn't actually produce income from that opportunity doesn't earn the commission. Of course, that happens sometimes, but it shouldn't happen a lot. Agreed?

By the same token, a sales leader who succeeds in getting a hire to walk in the door but who doesn't get that salesperson to a point where they are consistently hitting their numbers and choosing to stick around does not get credit for bringing a real contributor on board. Yes, early departures and major performance challenges do happen from time to time, but they shouldn't happen a lot. That's just as obvious as in the above paragraph, isn't it?

If you're a sales leader, it is essential that your talent pipeline includes not just the people you decide could be a good fit with your team or those to whom you make a job offer but also the people you successfully onboard and develop. Your hiring "deal" is not closed until the salesperson is up and running and producing income at mutually agreed-upon levels. Getting the salesperson to that point requires an engagement process, and planning the new sales hire's first weeks and months on the job is an essential part of that process.

Onboarding is the beginning of engagement—and, according to a recent Gallup report on the state of the American workplace, "Highly engaged business units achieve a 10% increase in customer metrics and a 20% increase in sales."[4]

There are four common, expensive mistakes sales leaders make when it comes to onboarding salespeople. Let's look at them now.

Mistake 1: Believing that onboarding takes care of itself. Unfortunately, many sales leaders adopt a "hire and forget" approach during this critical period, often justifying their actions with rationalizations like, "I am looking for a self-starter," or "We only hire smart people, and they can figure it out." These rationalizations sabotage the onboarding process and, very often, succeed only in pointing good talent toward your competition. Even the best sales hire needs a clear written roadmap for success, resources that support that journey, specific dates for attaining key performance benchmarks, and strong, consistent direction from the sales leader in the crucial weeks when they are deciding whether or not they want to commit to this team. A lot of avoiding Mistake 1 comes down to effective coaching (a topic covered in Rule 4), and creating the right playbooks (discussed in Rule 13).

Mistake 2: Acting as though onboarding only begins once an offer to work at your company has been made. This is a little like saying that the sales process begins with the handshake that confirms the verbal agreement. Onboarding is about supporting the relationship. The person's relationship with your company starts during the interview process. That means an essential part of the onboarding occurs during interviews, too. If your goal is to recruit the very best talent, and it should be, you will want to use the interview phase not just to confirm a match with your SEARCH profile but also to set appropriate expectations every step of the way. This gives the candidate a clear sense of what success will look like, especially in the early days, and to introduce the potential hire to peers and colleagues you trust, so they can do some interviewing and share their recommendations with you before the job offer is extended.*

Mistake 3: Imagining that onboarding is just for the new hire. The onboarding process is as much for you as it is for the new hire. Why? Because you are the one who must monitor the behaviors and the performance numbers during the crucial early days. There needs to be agreement on the behavioral plan and on the key performance indicators (KPIs) you will both be paying attention to.

Below, you'll find a list of the typical top-ten sales behaviors for most salespeople. During the ramp-up period that follows the hire, you will probably want to monitor at least five of these behaviors closely as KPIs and elevate two or three as special priorities for ongoing discussion with the new hire. Choosing one of these ten areas to focus on and identifying strategies for measurable improvement is a good goal for each coaching session with a new sales hire—or, for that matter, with any of your team. (See Rule 4, on coaching.)

1. **Lead generation:** Prospecting, the #1 behavior that drives all the others.

* When it comes to interviewing salespeople, excluding peers and colleagues from the process is a classic error. Getting the input of other people should be considered an essential prerequisite of any good sales hire.

2. **Building relationships:** Establishing strong, open relationships based on trust.
3. **Qualifying opportunity:** Determining a reason to do business.
4. **Making presentations:** Presenting solutions to the prospect's problems.
5. **Servicing customers:** Delivering superior customer satisfaction.
6. **Account management:** Maximizing business in each account.
7. **Territory development:** Building a strategy to grow the territory.
8. **Building or revising a Cookbook for Success*:** Establishing a behavioral plan that supports productive sales activity.
9. **Continuous education:** Developing ongoing product, market, and sales knowledge.

* Sandler's Cookbook for Success is a proven list of activities and behaviors that ensure success for salespeople. It should be set the moment new hire starts, and refined based on the data the new hire generates once on the job. For more information please visit www.sandler.com/blog/inside-sales-tip-use-cookbook.

10. **Execution of the selling system:** Mastering the team's documented sales process.

Note: If you don't have a sales process that is documented and consistent across the team and that each team member can describe and execute accurately, then you must fix that problem first.

Mistake 4: Not setting clear behavioral goals. What specific behavioral targets does the new hire need to hit over the first 30 days on the job? The first 60 days? The first 90 days? Many sales leaders make the mistake of simply focusing on income goals. The onboarding period is the time when you must identify, discuss, track, and troubleshoot the new hire's progress toward the most important behavioral goals, not just the deals that close.

This is an essential part of winning buy-in and creating engagement with the new hire. Make sure they know exactly what they need to do when in order to achieve success, and then support them as they do that. Note: If you are recruiting top sales talent and you cannot explain exactly how you plan to make the person successful by helping them create a behavioral plan that ramps them up quickly, then someone else will—and you will lose that salesperson to the competition.

SALES LEADERSHIP KEYS: RULE 3

7. Manage the recruitment phase of your pipeline strategically.
8. Avoid the most common onboarding mistakes.

RULE 4

Model and Coach Excellence with Private Meetings

USE ONE-ON-ONE DISCUSSIONS TO SUPPORT GROWTH AND DEVELOPMENT.

"A lot of people notice when you succeed, but they don't see what it took to get there."

—Dawn Staley

WHEN ASKED ONCE about the beginnings of his career, the great comic actor Gene Wilder told a story about his response as a young boy to his mother's heart attack. Wilder was only eight years old when she came home from the hospital, and of course he was frightened and disoriented. The doctor took the shell-shocked child aside and said something that would change his life forever. He leaned in and whispered, "Don't ever get into an argument with your mother, because you might kill her. Try to make her laugh."

The one thing Wilder knew for sure was that he didn't want to lose his mother. In that instant, the child realized he had some growing up to do and that he had to do that growing up in a hurry. Wilder had never consciously tried to make anyone laugh before in his life, but he did try from that moment on. And he succeeded. He made his mother laugh, she recovered from the heart attack, and she lived for years. Who can say whether her son's sense of humor was the reason? It certainly didn't hurt.

I tell you this story not to encourage you to make your salespeople laugh (although that's great if you can do it appropriately), but to share a much deeper challenge. I want you to consider the possibility that sales leaders, too, have an obligation to grow up in a hurry. Why? Because you don't want to lose good people. Although lives may not be at risk, your ability to attract, retain, and motivate good, talented employees is always at risk. That means you have to look closely at your priorities. You have to find a way to remind yourself, constantly, that effective leadership is not about you.

Effective leadership is not about arguments. It is not about settling scores, airing grievances, or proving who is right and who is wrong. It is about conversations that make sure salespeople are safe, engaged, committed to the mission, and productive. That kind of conversation is the opposite of an argument. This part of the book explains how to have more and more of those kinds of conversations with your team. Some of those conversations may be difficult; some will be easy. But none of them should give your people the workplace equivalent of a heart attack.

Like Gene Wilder, you need to realize what the most important priorities are. You simply can't afford to degrade, destroy, or ignore critical relationships. You need to support them. The single best opportunity you have for protecting and deepening your relationship with your direct reports is one that is woefully underutilized in today's workplace: the private, one-on-one meeting. In this chapter, you'll learn how to use that meeting to make it all about them—not about you.

There are two kinds of one-on-one meetings we advise sales leaders to schedule with their salespeople. Both give you the opportunity to walk your talk—that is, to demonstrate that you value what you say you value, that you are committed to supporting the other person, and that you are willing and able to initiate and sustain Adult-to-Adult interactions that strengthen the relationship. Let's look first at the easiest of those two meetings, the weekly check-in.

SALES LEADERSHIP KEY 9: SCHEDULE A WEEKLY CHECK-IN.

The weekly check-in is a brief, no-drama connection that can take place virtually or in person and usually lasts between five and fifteen minutes. It's important to have such a discussion at least once a week with every salesperson who reports to you directly.

There are five important things for you to cover during these regularly scheduled one-on-one meetings. They are summarized below. A side note: If you cover these points regularly and predictably and if you also make a habit of sending them your agenda well ahead of time, you can establish a predictable ongoing cadence with each salesperson. The nice thing about such a cadence is that it allows you both to use your (limited) time efficiently, without either of you having to "wait for the download." People will know what to expect and prepare ahead of time for the meeting.

1. **Set your up-front contract.** Get agreement on the purpose of the discussion, the time allotted, and the specific issues or questions that each person wants to address. You will probably also want to confirm that there will be no interruptions. (By the way, the salesperson should be setting exactly the same kind of contract with their prospects, so be sure you effectively model up-front contract best practices here.)

2. **Look at what's working.** Always start with positive reinforcement. Briefly focus on something positive the person did since your last meeting. Offer authentic, heartfelt praise.

Don't offer fake praise—that will undermine the bonding and rapport necessary for a good check-in meeting. Many managers look at one-on-one meetings as an excuse to closely evaluate mistakes the salesperson made. That's a meeting nobody looks forward to. By focusing on something the salesperson did well, you ensure the behavior will be repeated. A good sequence of questions that we share with sales leaders to use during weekly check-ins is:

"What are you currently doing well?"
"What could you be doing better?"
"What could you be doing differently?"

It is essential to let the salespeople come up with their own answers to these questions.

3. **Discuss the last meeting's action items and preview items for this week.** Follow through and check in on the status of any specific commitments the salesperson made to you during your last meeting. Identify any to-do items you want to be sure the person accomplishes before your next meeting.
4. **Talk about the behaviors.** Your report should have a clear behavioral plan outlining specific, measurable activities that they are committed to performing on a daily and weekly basis. Think of this as a cookbook—a tested, repeatable

recipe for success.* For instance: How many voice-to-voice conversations with new contacts should the salesperson initiate each week? How many referral requests should the salesperson make from current customers? How many presentations to qualified decision makers—that is to say, people who have a problem that your company can solve, a budget that will allow the prospect and your company to work together, and transparency about their decision-making process—are expected? These numbers should be part of a mutually agreed-upon weekly behavioral plan that supports both the salesperson's income goal and the team income goal. Examine the performance numbers together. Discuss their implications for the achievement of the most important goals when the measured behaviors are extrapolated over the month, quarter, and year.

5. **Get a clear verbal commitment.** Near the end of this brief meeting, you will probably have identified one or two particularly important things that you definitely want to see some action on before the two of you get together again. In the moments before you wrap up, set expectations by asking for a clear verbal commitment that the salesperson will take action on in these one or two critical

* See footnote in Sales Leadership Key 8.

areas. Hearing the salesperson speak the actual words is important. When people commit to something verbally, they are far more likely to get it done.

This, then, is the first kind of one-on-one meeting you should have with salespeople who report to you. The goal is always to support the person and make sure they have what they need to do the job. It's probably a good idea to consider these weekly check-ins non-negotiable parts of working for you.

Remember: Adults learn by imitation and illustration. It's easier for them to perform a task at the highest level of excellence when they can see you doing it on a regular basis. The main thing you are modeling as a leader is good Adult-to-Adult communication—communication that is free of games and free of blame. The weekly check-in meeting you just read about is a superb opportunity to model that kind of communication.

Let's look now at a more intricate, more demanding, and lengthier meeting: the coaching meeting.

SALES LEADERSHIP KEY 10: HOLD COACHING MEETINGS.

Although both must be conducted in private, a coaching meeting* is very different from a weekly check-in meeting. A check-in meeting is focused on short-term commitments and

* In much of what follows, I am indebted to Bill Bartlett's fine book, *The Sales Coach's Playbook*.

outcomes; a coaching session is part of a much longer process that supports the salesperson's long-term personal and professional development.

According to the Institute of Coaching, over 70% of individuals who receive coaching benefited from improved work performance, better relationships, and more effective communication skills.[5]

In fact, if you are serious about becoming a true coach by taking on the responsibility of leading this kind of sensitive private meeting, it is important to understand that coaching is not an isolated event. Rather, it's a process of ongoing discovery that you as the coach support and facilitate, usually by asking questions that the salesperson has not yet considered.

Often, coaching fails because it is seen as a "one and done" session where change is supposed to take place instantaneously. That is not what this meeting is meant to do. The coaching meeting aims to help the direct report determine what needs to happen next, and why, at this point in their life and in their career. Think of this as a series of ongoing conversations, not as a single "fix it" session. Always remember: This is about them, not you.

What we are talking about, then, is a dramatic deepening of the working relationship between you and your direct report by means of a series of discussions that helps the person further develop strengths and overcome weak areas. This kind of relationship unfolds not in one or two intense crisis-management sessions but through consistent, ongoing interaction—perhaps every two weeks. It is a mistake to try to make this discussion about fixing any short-term problem you identify as the sales leader.

The goal of coaching is continuous growth of the salesperson, on their own terms, over a measured period of time.

Coaching salespeople requires discovery-based thinking from both sides. In this kind of thinking, people open their minds and determine their own solutions to any problems, and the coach supports that process. The best coaching sessions involve the salesperson discovering for themselves new ways to modify existing behavior to achieve an outcome that is personally important to them. This is, of course, impossible when the person does not feel safe, so an early priority is the creation of a nurturing, nonjudgmental environment for the coaching conversation. The coach must develop a "safe zone" of deep mutual trust that enables both parties to have candid conversations.

The three critical elements to understand during each coaching session are *what*, *reason*, and *importance*. The *what* is the shared purpose of the coaching session, which should be something personally important to the direct report*; the *reason* is why it is necessary to achieve the mutually agreed-upon goal; and the *importance* is the real-world impact the accomplishment will have for the direct report. Successful coaches are able to establish all three of these elements early in coaching relationships and use them to measure the level of trust the person has in them. Trust is a key factor driving success and can be measured using the same symbols used in the Olympics: gold, silver, and bronze.

Gold-level trust is achieved over time. This must be your ultimate goal. The most productive coaching sessions involve the highest level of trust between participants. This high level of trust fosters internal exploration through openness and vulnerability and speeds growth and development. Silver-level trust is what exists when there is the potential for growth but there is not yet complete openness and vulnerability. Bronze-level trust exists when there are no known barriers to constructive interaction but the coaching relationship has only just begun. This, in all likelihood, is where you and the salesperson will be during the first coaching session.

---

* One possible purpose for a coaching session with a salesperson is improvement in one of the top ten sales behaviors discussed in Rule 3. However, if this is the *what* for the meeting, it is imperative that the salesperson consider improvement of that behavior to be a personal priority, in support of a unique personal goal that is important for them to attain. The coach thinking the salesperson needs improvement in that area is not sufficient.

Most successful coaches conduct two forms of coaching sessions: strategic and tactical. Strategic coaching focuses on helping salespeople plan for success in the long term. Tactical coaching helps them understand the skills and execution traps currently preventing them from greater success. Note that tactical coaching does not equate to, "Here, watch me do it!"

In both strategic and tactical coaching, the #1 focus of the coach is to ask critical questions in order to help the participant fully understand the issues driving the coaching session. Most managers, in our experience, if they coach at all, tend to do only tactical coaching. They are coaching to address a single issue or problem, but they are not setting the employee up for sustainable growth and success over time.

Advanced questioning skills are key to successful strategic and tactical coaching sessions. They help the coach avoid the trap of "telling/fixing." The coach's best friend is active listening. The simple query, "Tell me more," gets the information ball rolling and allows the participant to "play a movie" of key events and decisions.

Active listening is the process of reflecting back to the speaker the message you heard in order to confirm or correct your understanding. It can be accomplished by summarizing the speaker's message and asking for confirmation or clarification as needed. Active listening not only facilitates effective communication but also enhances rapport and builds trust. Of course, this is true not only in coaching situations but in all your interactions with salespeople.

The Sandler concepts of reversing (answering a question with a question) as well as strip-lining (presenting an idea that is the opposite of the one your conversational partner expects to hear) play significant roles in gathering the information needed to help the participant achieve the desired strategic or tactical outcome. This kind of engagement keeps the focus on the person's understanding of the situation. It is vitally important for the coach to listen without prejudice and judgment in order to accurately reflect back to the salesperson what is being said. The coach must block all predetermined opinions about the situation or the person, since they will skew the results of the session.

Note that the salesperson must take full responsibility for executing any new behaviors discussed in the coaching session. These actions should be specifically summed up at the session's end.

The success of both of these private meetings will depend heavily upon your ability to identify your direct report's most important personal goals and then align them with the goals of the team and the organization. This is the topic of Rule 5, which we will cover next.

SALES LEADERSHIP KEYS: RULE 4

9. Schedule a weekly check-in.
10. Hold coaching meetings.

RULE 5

Tap Into the *Why*

FIND OUT WHAT DRIVES PEOPLE ON A PERSONAL LEVEL.

"To live a fulfilled life, we need to keep creating the 'what is next' of our lives. Without dreams and goals there is no living, only merely existing, and that is not why we are here."

—Mark Twain

IMAGINE ASKING A FRIEND to pull up the GPS app on their phone so they can use the app to find you and meet you at a nice coffee shop you've just discovered. The cafe is easy to miss; it's in an obscure part of town neither of you have ever visited before.

Now imagine that, when your friend agrees and asks for the name of the coffee shop and the cross streets so they can find the location and plug it into the GPS, you text back instead, "See you in fifteen minutes." And wait for your friend to materialize.

Half an hour goes by. Then an hour. Then two.

Imagine that you then call your friend and ask, in an irritated tone, "Why aren't you here? I thought we were going to have coffee!"

Would your friend be at fault? Or would you?

Of course, there was no way for your friend to join you for coffee—they didn't know where they were supposed to go. Here's the challenge that little story connects to: Sales leaders sometimes fall into the trap of believing that, since they know where they want to go, everyone else knows the destination, too—and wants to get there and has all the tools necessary to do so. This is what happens when you hand someone a business goal but you don't take the trouble to explain the goal, discuss the right benchmarks, find out where they need help, and then align your business goal with what's really most important, on a human level, to that individual. By leaving them in the lurch, you leave them behind.

When they don't hit the goal, you may feel frustrated, but the truth of the matter is, if you never put the goal into terms that mattered to them or were even comprehensible to them, you can't expect much else. It's the equivalent of expecting them to materialize at a certain spot at a certain time without telling them the cross streets.

Leaders often make the mistake of fixating on what they are trying to make happen and on their own reasons for why it ought to happen. They may spend much less time trying to figure out the big personal *why* that will motivate someone on their sales team to pitch in and make it happen. That won't work. People will work a lot harder for their own goals—their family, their community, their own well-being—than they will ever work for a boss.

SALES LEADERSHIP KEY 11: LEARN WHAT YOUR REPORTS WANT IN THEIR LIVES.

Executing on this Sales Leadership Key means taking the time to invite a salesperson who reports to you out for some one-on-one time. Ask them to lunch; take an hour or so to talk with them about what is happening in their world—and also about what they would like to have happen in their world. The ground rules for this conversation are simple: No shop talk. No monopolizing the floor. No turning the conversation's direction to what you want. Make this hour all about getting to know this salesperson on a personal level.

At the end of the hour, you should be able to identify at least one, and perhaps two or three, nonwork initiatives that are important to that person as an individual, not as an employee. Are they hoping to get their kids through college without saddling them with a huge debt load? Are they struggling with difficult decisions about how to take care of an aging parent? Are they working on writing the great American novel? Do they want to take a month off for a vacation in Tibet?

If a salesperson reports directly to you, you should have some idea of the big challenges and the big aspirations they're facing in life outside of the workplace, because that's what they're working toward. If you don't take the time to identify those things, that's a failure of leadership. Unfortunately, it's an extremely common failure. When I ask groups of leaders to raise their hands if they can identify one important nonwork-related goal of one direct report, I rarely see a single hand go up. That's a gap that you need to close, if only because you can't possibly help them align professional goals with personal goals if you don't even know what their personal goals are. Simply throwing a numerical target at someone gives them no reason to set up a plan or to execute that plan. You have to figure out their big *why* first, and connect what they do at work to that big *why*. Then, encourage them to write the big personal goal down—and to talk about the goal regularly. Formalizing the goal in this way can lead to real breakthroughs.

In a 2020 study led by researcher Michaela Schippers, students who committed personal goals to writing showed a 22% increase in academic performance when compared with students who did not put their goals in writing. The increase showed up even when the goals students wrote about had nothing to do with academics.[6]

SALES LEADERSHIP KEY 12: ONCE YOU KNOW THEIR BIG *WHY*, CONNECT THE DOTS.

If you know what the person's big *why* is and you are willing to think creatively, you can find all kinds of good ways to tie the workplace performance to the attainment of that person's goal. You can help them set up a behavioral plan that supports their reaching the business goal. You can set up an incentive plan that delivers the reward that makes the personal goal visible, viable, and attainable. (Note that this new incentive arrangement may mean looking at things other than money, such as flexible hours, developmental and educational resources, or promotional opportunities.) You can figure out the metrics that connect their behaviors to both the business plan and the change they want to see take place in their life. But first, you have to help people connect the dots on an emotional level. They have to believe the attainment of their goal is a realistic event, as something possible in their world.

Let me share with you my favorite example of all time illustrating what this connect-the-dots process looks like in action. David Sandler went through this process with me and figured out that I wanted a particular car—a luxury vehicle. Now, this particular car cost more than I could even imagine myself paying for a car at the time. So what did Sandler do? He drove me to the dealership. He made sure I got to see and test drive the car.

He didn't stop there. As it happened, Sandler had a very similar car. One day, I was about to head out the door, getting ready to take a prospect to lunch, when he stopped me. He told me to drive his car to the lunch meeting.

He said it very casually: "Hey, why don't you take my car?" But I knew it was not a request, and I also knew what he was doing. He wanted me to have the emotional experience of driving a luxury car to that big meeting. He wanted to motivate me. You know what? I didn't care. I liked being motivated. I drove the car to the meeting—and I enjoyed every minute of the drive.

Sandler wasn't done yet. He made the car part of our coaching discussions. He made sure that it showed up on my list of goals. He mentioned the car frequently. He even gave me a picture of the car I wanted. He said, "Put this on your bathroom mirror. Every morning when you get up, you'll look at it. When you look at this picture, it's going to remind you every day that this is what you're working toward. Stare at that picture long enough, and it will start to grind at you. You're going to do whatever you can to get there."

Sure enough, he was right. Pretty soon, I came up with some creative ways to generate revenue for the company that made extra commissions for me, ways that I would never have come up with if he hadn't connected with my big *why*. I kept getting creative until I had achieved the goal. Within a year of the day he first suggested I drive his luxury car, my luxury car was in my driveway. Why? Because my boss had helped me connect the dots. He'd made sure that I was going after that car. That's the power of connecting the dots. You and your team can experience the emotion of attaining a goal, just like Dave helped me to experience it.

So take the age-old concept of visualization and apply it in your team's world. What is most important to your direct reports on a personal level? What is it they want to make happen? Is it a wedding, or a great retirement, or a vacation home? Whatever it is, help them connect the dots. Help them find pictures that will make the goal real for them ahead of time. When they put those visuals on their bathroom mirrors or in their workstations and they look at them day after day, they will be motivated—and they will go the extra mile.

SALES LEADERSHIP KEYS: RULE 5

11. Learn what your reports want in their lives.
12. Once you know their big *why*, connect the dots.

RULE 6

Begin with Their Point of View

UNDERSTAND AND RESPECT BEHAVIORAL STYLE AND PERSPECTIVE.

"Always remember that you are absolutely unique. Just like everyone else."

—Margaret Mead

PEOPLE SEE THE WORLD through their own sunglasses. When you expect them to see the world through yours, there are inevitably problems.

You may not see those problems right away, but they are there. When you try to coach someone on your team under the assumption that they see the world in exactly the same way you do—and that they have (or should have) the exact same experiences and competencies that you have—there are going to be missteps. These missteps might cause resentments and hurt feelings. The salesperson may conceal it for a time, but eventually those resentments and hurt feelings will rise to the surface.

Each employee brings to the table a unique set of experiences, needs, and capacity to contribute. The salespeople on your team are not identical building blocks for you to stack and unstack and stack again as you see fit. Nor are they pieces of equipment you can take out of a box, use to achieve your business objectives, then put back in the box. They are people—real live human beings with their own stories, their own aspirations, their own communication styles, and their own special competencies. When you act as though they are all basically the same, they see that as a lack of respect—and they are right to do so.

In the prior chapter, you learned that it is your job as the sales leader to uncover the salesperson's most important goals and to find a way to align those goals with your business objectives. Now it's time to take the next step. It's also your job to make sure that you understand the communication styles and competencies of everyone on your team. It's your job to be flexible in communicating with the members of the team, because you want to get the very best out of your people. Being flexible enough to learn how people naturally communicate and what they have to offer is the only realistic way to inspire them to do their best. It's not the salesperson's job to learn how to get the very best out of you—it's the other way around.

SALES LEADERSHIP KEY 13: UNDERSTAND DISC.

If you have children, you already know that every child is different. You simply can't miss noticing this fact as they grow up. Kids see things and experience things in radically different ways from each other—which is one of the reasons they so often get into heated disagreements that parents have to step in and referee.

Think about it. Children can sometimes evaluate relationships and situations so differently from each other that they sometimes seem to be living in entirely different worlds. They often feel quite passionate about the accuracy of their personal evaluations of what's happening in their world. This is part of the growth process, not just for them, but for their parents.

Parents need to see those different perspectives and understand them for what they are. It's an amazing gift to watch children who were raised under the same roof act with such striking variations in response to similar, or even identical, events. Some parents may find that they connect more naturally with one child than with another. They may think, "I like the way that child thinks." Why does this kind of thing happen? It may be because the child's way of thinking is the same as the parent's way of thinking. Or it may be because the child thinks about something that would never have occurred to the parent.

Guess what? That happens with your team members as well.

They have starkly different ways of assessing their surroundings, behaving, and interacting, just like kids do. Another way of stating this basic fact of human nature is that both kids and members of the sales team can display sharply differing behavioral styles.

This fact leads us to one of the best tools for analyzing behavioral styles: DISC.* DISC assessments, either done informally or carefully quantified, are based on psychologist William Moulton Marston's landmark 1928 theory about behavioral traits. This theory held that human beings tend to favor one of four basic behavioral patterns, summarized in the chart on the next page. See if any of the groups match up with people you know. Which one best describes you?

* Nobody "owns" DISC, although there are more and less reliable sources for conducting the assessments that will help you to determine, with a high degree of accuracy, who shows up where in the DISC matrix. We have delivered great results for our clients over the years working with a company called Extended DISC.

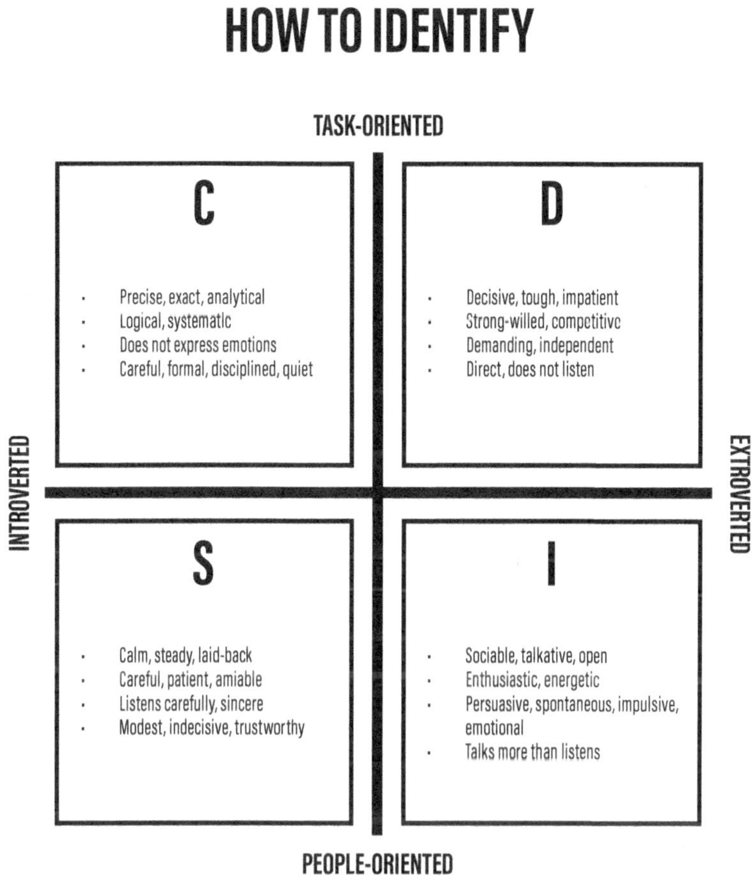

Notice anyone you recognize? Most people do. The point is, each of those boxes represents a distinct behavioral "language." Most people only speak one of these languages—their own. High Dominants, for instance, are usually most comfortable communicating with other Dominants—those types of folks agree on getting to the point and taking action. If you can learn to speak beyond your own "default" language, if you can learn to speak—and listen—in all four styles, your potential to influence others and to support your team expands dramatically.*

Here are four different sales leaders, each representing a specific DISC style. While each leader is talking about the same project, notice how different the priorities and the voices are. Which is closest to your voice?

- **High Dominant:** "We need to get the team together and attack this new opportunity with Acme International. If we get this right, we can increase our revenues by 30% this quarter. So let's assemble the right lineup, figure out what the best practices are, and get this moving. We want to implement the very best ideas we can, as soon as we can, so please forget about the politics, pick the very best people, and move this forward for me. I want to see a plan, and I want it implemented within three days."
- **High Influencer:** "This project is a great opportunity for us to get closer to Acme International. We all know how important the voice of the customer is, and we all want to find new ways to get deeper clarity about the customer's point of view. So with all that in mind, let's start the

* I should point out here that a fairly small percentage of people—me, for instance—tend to operate intermittently out of two DISC styles. In my case, it's Dominant and Compliant. For such people, it's particularly important to be able to communicate based on what you know about the modality they're using at any given moment.

discussion and begin thinking about the best ways for us to move this project forward."

- **High Steady Relator:** "When I was asked to participate in this project, I suggested that we get feedback from all the departments currently working with Acme International about our objective before we proceed. It is very important to get everyone's input, so that each team has a voice. So let's take this a step at a time. Remember we need to figure out if something is working before we rush ahead and change something that doesn't need changing. Also, I think we should beta test whatever initiative we do come up with before we try to roll it out at full scale."
- **High Compliant:** "Before we even begin, we need to think this opportunity with Acme International through. What's the end game supposed to look like? Based on that, what are the key benchmarks going to be, and what are the roles and responsibilities going to be to deliver the results we want? Business is business. Let's make sure we are only making logical decisions as we move forward to expand our profile within Acme."

You should know before we go any further that there is no right or wrong DISC style. There is no one right way to launch a project. But there is the opportunity to ask yourself:

"Which voice is closest to mine?"

"How can I avoid the mistake of thinking that the three other voices are somehow flawed?"

According to Extended DISC, the global breakdown of dominant DISC styles[7] is as follows:

- **Dominant 12%**
- **Influencer 30%**
- **Steady Relator 30%**
- **Compliant 28%**

Looking closely at the DISC model inevitably means looking closely at your own behavioral preferences. First and foremost, you will want to figure out where you land in the matrix—what your own DISC style is. That will help you to get better at identifying the styles of others, styles that you can then recognize and accommodate.

Let's say you are a High Dominant. Your instinct during meetings is to get right to the point as soon as possible, focus like a laser beam on the outcome or decision that you want the meeting to deliver, and then take action. Your message to everyone else: Get on the train! It's leaving the station!

Now, indulging that powerful instinct to jump right in, identify the problem, and quickly decide what to do about it would be you speaking the Dominant's language. I get it—it's tempting to keep speaking the language you're most familiar with and get right down to business as the meeting starts. Maybe you can win back five minutes in your working day by keeping all that boring social chitchat to an absolute bare minimum.

But what if the five-person team you are working with during this meeting consists of three Influencers and two Steady Relators?

Asking these people to skip the social chitchat is a little like asking them not to breathe. They will spend the entire meeting feeling like something is missing. You may find that you are able to get much more done as a group if you take just a few minutes at the top of the meeting to connect with the team members on an emotional level and let them connect with each other. Does this come naturally to you? Maybe not. Can you learn to do it? Absolutely. Let them express, briefly, what's going on in their world on a personal or family level; share what's going on in yours. You may just find that playing to their behavioral style in this way for a few minutes deepens your connection and your rapport with each individual team member and with the group as a whole—and makes it easier for you to work together as a group to create solutions that benefit everyone.

Here is a thumbnail sketch of some of the best ways to begin to broaden your DISC "vocabulary"—by moving beyond your own behavioral style to accommodate the styles of others.

When dealing with a Task Oriented/Extroverted **DOMINANT** • Be concise and focused in your communications with this team member. • Avoid rambling and chitchat. • Be open to this person aiding in the decision-making process rather than coming to them with the decision already made. • When disagreeing, ensure that you disagree with the facts in the matter instead of directing your disagreement at the individual.	When dealing with a Socially Oriented/Extroverted **INFLUENCER** • Be personable, and warm up the conversation with a little chitchat. At the same time, don't allow the main purpose of communication to become completely derailed. • Follow up in writing. • When discussing ideas with this person, support your point of view with testimonials given by people that this particular staff member admires or respects.
When dealing with a Task Oriented/Introverted **COMPLIANT** • Prepare organized, concise supporting evidence before speaking with this employee about new ideas or changes. • Lead by example, and always follow through on what you've said you'll do. • Be especially careful about respecting personal space during face-to-face conversations with this DISC type.	When dealing with a Socially Oriented/Introverted **STEADY RELATOR** • Similar to the Influencer, this employee needs a little friendly conversation before leading into the business portion of the conversation. • After talking to this person, be sure to listen to what they have to say. Play it back so the person knows you've heard and understood. • Provide this person with time to think things through if that is requested. This person does not like to be rushed or forced into a decision. • Stay true to your word, avoiding empty promises or exaggerations. That's good advice for everyone, of course, but it's particularly important if you expect to maintain this person's trust.

SALES LEADERSHIP KEY 14: INVEST IN ASSESSMENTS.

It's a good idea to do formal assessments of each member of your sales team to figure out exactly which DISC profile they are operating from and what their key competencies are.*

We usually recommend that leaders also conduct formal assessments of sales team member competencies, core values, and behaviors that are not covered by the DISC model, such as:

- Work ethic.
- Planning.
- Taking the initiative and acting independently.
- Managing change.
- Solving problems.
- Making decisions.
- Taking appropriate risks.
- Innovating.
- Communicating effectively.
- Building and maintaining relationships over time.

These are vitally important factors when it comes to matching the right team members with the right assignments—and,

* Again, we recommend the company Extended DISC for this.

for that matter, evaluating prospective sales hires. If you are resistant to the idea of investing in such assessments, maybe ask yourself: Do doctors let patients self-diagnose when it comes to determining whether they are healthy or they need to make some lifestyle changes? Do they let patients self-diagnose the illness they are suffering from? Of course not. Does it make any more sense to self-diagnose when it comes to your personnel assignments, your hires, and your development plans? An outside expert assessment is invaluable.*

SALES LEADERSHIP KEY 15: USE DIFFERENT MODALITIES.

It's easy to forget that salespeople respond differently to different communication platforms. Whether you're communicating with a single team member or with the team as a whole, you have to make sure that you're sending the right messages and ensuring they are delivered in the right way and with the right frequency in order for them to have the biggest impact.

You may be most comfortable sending email after email about important issues. Email is great, if the team members are the type of people who read emails. But in today's world, where many salespeople are working remotely, we find that people are often bombarded with so many different types of communication that

* Our chosen partner for these competency-focused assessments is OutMatch.

it's hard to keep up. You may want to consider reinforcing major emails with a video, explaining what's going on, and even having team videoconferences to make sure the message gets through. Podcasts and webinars are also great communication tools.

The best sales leaders, I've noticed, hit every modality multiple times. When they're presenting important information that everyone needs to be aware of—something that you might expect a salesperson to be able to absorb in a few minutes—they continue messaging about it using multiple platforms for weeks or even months, just to make certain it's seen and understood. As an example: I send a weekly video to our employees and another weekly video to the 256 Sandler offices around the world. On occasion, I also will record a Zoom message and send it to a committee or even to an individual. That's often faster and easier than calling a meeting, and it's a great way to say exactly what I want to say, in the way I want to say it, with a minimal time investment. Just as important, I know people will watch the content.

SALES LEADERSHIP KEYS: RULE 6

13. Understand DISC.
14. Invest in assessments.
15. Use different modalities.

RULE 7

Be Strategically Inquisitive

ASK QUESTIONS THAT CLARIFY ALL THE IMPORTANT ISSUES.

"It is a capital mistake to theorize before one has data. Insensibly one begins to twist facts to suit theories, instead of theories to suit facts."

—**Sherlock Holmes**, "A Scandal in Bohemia"
by Arthur Conan Doyle (1891)

SHERLOCK HOLMES IS ONE of the most enduringly popular literary creations in human history. Well over a hundred and thirty years after his first appearance in the London magazine *Beeton's Christmas Annual*, and nearly a century after the death of his creator Arthur Conan Doyle, audiences and readers are still endlessly fascinated by Mr. Holmes, buying books, watching films, and turning on television shows that share his adventures. The Guinness Book of World Records has designated Holmes as the "most portrayed literary human character" in mass media.

Why so much fascination for this character?

I believe Holmes's inextinguishable popularity has to do with a remarkable trait of his that speaks to something deep within the human psyche, a trait that connects to a person's own survival and the survival of the community. It is this: He is endlessly curious about his environment.

Holmes is always seeking out possible connections that others might have missed, always posing questions that others fail to ask, always noticing details others consider unimportant. He is compelled to gather and evaluate data. Faced with some deep mystery that baffles the police, he is totally committed to the goal of gathering all available information so he can draw relevant, accurate conclusions. As a result, he almost always solves the case before him. He is curious with a purpose—relentlessly, strategically inquisitive.

Truly great sales leaders, in my experience, have this same trait. They don't assume they have all the answers. They never stop looking for clues. They look around all the corners. They never ignore important sources of information or potential truth, even when these come from the most unlikely sources. They don't hang on tight to a single reality filter. They move their minds around roadblocks, such as who said it, what people think of that person, whether the person has been wrong before, and so on. Everyone has an opinion and a potential piece of the puzzle to pass along. The leader's job is to put the pieces together so they can identify the best possible answer. That means gathering the most possible data.

In this chapter, we'll look at some strategies you can use to emulate Sherlock Holmes so that you, like him, can put all the pieces together and crack whatever case is before you.

SALES LEADERSHIP KEY 16: BE PRESENT FOR EVERY CONVERSATION.

Human ears can accept up to 500 words per minute, but human mouths can only speak at 100–150 words per minute. If you think about that, that's a sizeable gap. The big question sales leaders face is what are you going to do with all that extra mind space?

Too many sales leaders will go on mental vacations waiting for the other person to get to the point. They might disengage from the salesperson who is right in front of them and start thinking about other people, other issues, other problems. They may tell themselves they're "multitasking" (particularly if the conversation is not playing out in the same physical space), but that's a convenient fiction. The truth is, they're either doing something else or having private conversations with themselves, when they could be connecting with the person they're talking to. Think back to the last time you said to a salesperson, "Could you say that again?" Was the issue that you didn't understand what the person was saying? Or was it that your mind was somewhere else?

Research suggests that many people quickly forget the vast majority of what they hear from others. A 2018 study conducted by researchers Sarah Brown-Schmidt and Aaron S. Benjamin found that "after a short delay, conversational participants may recall from memory fewer than 20% of the specific ideas that were originally expressed."[8]

The first and most important key to being strategically inquisitive is to focus with full attention on the person in front of you. This is a critical leadership skill, and yes, it takes practice. You have to actually show up for the conversation. This is vitally important in all of your dealings, but it's particularly critical when you are interacting with salespeople. If you make time for them, you need to be fully present during that time.

Think about it from the other side. Your salesperson wants to share information. They want to be heard. They're sharing what they believe is relevant information. When you are distracted with something else and you are only giving them a fraction of your attention, they notice that. They interpret that as you telling them you either don't care what they're saying or that you don't care about them. You may not have intended to send those signals, but that's what you are conveying.

Remember Yoda's advice to Luke Skywalker in *The Empire Strikes Back*? "Do or do not. There is no try." This definitely applies to interpersonal communication. Whether you are online, on the phone, or in person, if you are asked to take part in a real-time conversation, you can either be 100% available during the time allotted or you can be honest and say that you need to be somewhere else. There is no middle ground.

SALES LEADERSHIP KEY 17: FOLLOW THE 70/30 RULE.

The 70/30 Rule originated as a guideline for salespeople, but it is just as essential for sales leaders.

All of the sales leaders we work with, without exception, tell us they want their salespeople to be great listeners. Listening is one of those skills they simply expect people to bring to the table. Yet we hear many of those same leaders saying, "I've explained such-and-such to them multiple times. Are they not even listening?" So here's a question to consider: Who is modeling the behavior of listening for them?

It's easy to forget that listening is also a best practice for leaders. In fact, it's one of the most important skills of all. There is a time and a place to give a speech, of course—but only when there's an audience of willing listeners.

David Sandler recommended that the seller talk no more than 30% of the time and that the buyer talk at least 70% of the time. That's why it's called the 70/30 Rule. Sandler used to tell salespeople that they had two ears and one mouth for a reason; it's a reminder to use them in that same proportion. This should be the standard for leaders, as well.

Why is this a challenge? Insecurity and chronic time compression often play major roles here. Even so, if you want to be truly effective, you may want to find a way to remind yourself to listen a little more and talk a little less. After all, you want your people to be self-sufficient. You don't want to create an atmosphere of learned helplessness, where your team comes to you for every decision or answer.

When you listen effectively, you ask good questions—questions that clarify exactly what the situation is. Ask questions that help your salespeople find the right path forward, the path that will allow them to take the next step toward proactively resolving their issue. Good listening is always based on asking relevant questions and not on giving instructions. Unfortunately, many sales leaders hear a problem or a question from a salesperson and immediately launch into a mode of communication that I call, "Here's the answer." The sales leader asks no questions at all, but simply says, "Do A, B, and C."

Now, did the salesperson just get an answer? Sure. Was it

something that they may be able to use? Maybe. Will they actually use it consistently in their daily life? Probably not. Why not? Because it was someone else's answer, not theirs.

Under pressure, people revert back to whatever they're accustomed to doing. When a leader just gives instructions, they don't do anything to change that pattern. But when a leader asks good questions and actually listens, they can help people come to their own conclusions about what they should be doing. That leads to a much higher probability that the salesperson will actually implement what is under discussion—because it feels like their own idea. By listening, you may also find ways to build some of the things the salesperson just said into your response, even further increasing the chances of implementation.

People don't argue with their own data—if they themselves said it, it must be true. If someone else says it, that same data could be suspect. The best sales leaders support people by helping them become motivated to reach their own conclusions and change their own behaviors.

Here's an example of challenging the salesperson to self-solve: "What would you have done about this problem if I had been out sick today?" The answer that comes back is usually very interesting, and it can lead you both toward a better and deeper conversation. Asking this kind of question, instead of simply stepping in and "solving the problem" is an essential part of supporting a self-correcting sales team—the kind of team that can scale its success as it grows.

SALES LEADERSHIP KEY 18: WHEN PEOPLE SPEAK UP, HELP THEM FEEL OK.

The instant you choose whether or not you are going to listen is the moment of truth for you as a leader. You either make salespeople feel OK for wanting to be heard, or you don't.

Everyone wants to be listened to; everybody wants to be heard. When people show up and explain their position or talk about a situation they are facing, they are often in self-discovery mode. They may be problem solving by talking things out. Great sales leaders recognize when that's happening and find ways to support that. How you respond is incredibly important, since you are the only one who can create an environment where salespeople feel comfortable talking through issues. Providing that safe environment is one of the most important parts of your job.

You may think you are making the environment safe for raising issues or posing questions, but it's harder to do this than you might imagine. Here's a classic example of what I mean.

Salesperson: Can I ask your opinion on something?

Sales Leader: Sure.

Salesperson: On the Acme project, I'm thinking of doing X. I'm just curious: Is that what you would do?

Sales Leader: Obviously, you should do X. That's the only way to do it. Don't waste your time with anything else.

You might not have noticed it, but that word "obviously" takes the sales leader into Critical Parent mode. Even though the leader was agreeing with the report, that word "obviously" instantly shut down the dialogue. Is that really the kind of conversation you want a salesperson to expect from you? It has the effect of making the salesperson less likely to reach out to you in the future when they are not absolutely certain about the best way forward. The answer may have been obvious to you, but if it were obvious to them, they wouldn't have asked.

It's better to find a way to praise them for reaching out for help. Then share, without judgment, exactly why you agree X is a good option, and, finally, ask about what other options they were considering. Who knows? They may have a better idea that they haven't shared with you yet, something you hadn't thought of.

SALES LEADERSHIP KEYS: RULE 7

16. Be present for every conversation.
17. Follow the 70/30 Rule.
18. When people speak up, make them feel OK.

RULE 8

Respect Their Truth

ACCEPT THAT YOURS IS NOT THE ONLY POINT OF VIEW AND THAT PEOPLE ARE JUST AS PASSIONATE ABOUT THEIR OPINION.

"Not everything that is faced can be changed, but nothing can be changed until it is faced."

—James Baldwin

HAVE YOU EVER RE-WATCHED a movie that you first saw weeks, months, or even years ago and realized how much more there was to appreciate than you saw the first time around? Did you pick up nuances from a film's story and characters the second time through, new shades of meaning, or even plot points that you might not have realized were there? It's possible, too, that a film you couldn't connect with at all on first viewing grew on you the second time you watched it—and left such a positive impression on you that you ended up recommending it to someone else.

Many people have experienced this. What's really fascinating to consider is the possibility that the person you were when you first watched the film is not identical to the person you were when you watched it the second time. That insight is particularly obvious when you watch a film at, say, age seventeen and then watch it again at age forty. But it's just as intriguing an outcome when you watch a film at age fifty and then watch it again at age fifty-one. The film stayed the same; what changed was your experiences, your perceptions, and your ability to process what was happening on the screen.

Why do I share this example? Simple: Sometimes people get so tied into their own perspective that they may convince themselves it is the only possible truth. Then, something happens to remind them that that's just not the case.

No one has the corner on the market when it comes to identifying the truth. First impressions about an event or situation are not always accurate. If you want to get a full picture before you make a decision, for example, you are well advised to seek out perspectives that differ from your own. That means taking other people's truth into consideration. It means making a conscious effort to evaluate their truth objectively, without assuming that your truth is somehow better or more valid than theirs—yours may not be. This is the big takeaway from a great management book I read years ago and have never forgotten, *Six Thinking Hats* by Edward de Bono. One of his main points was that the best leaders benefit by encouraging teams to challenge core assumptions and to evaluate multiple perspectives during their discussions.

The more perspectives you can elicit and take into account, the better your salespeople are going to feel about your willingness to listen to them—and the better your decisions are going to be. This chapter is all about getting more of those perspectives on the table for you to consider.

A classic study by Fodor and Smith suggested that leaders with "high power motivation" were more likely to create work environments in which teams reach consensus decisions without critical evaluation—a phenomenon known as "groupthink."[9]

SALES LEADERSHIP KEY 19: DON'T PREJUDGE ADVICE BASED ON WHO GAVE IT.

"Don't bother listening to that person—they're a jerk."

"Don't be surprised when this person complains—they come from a team that doesn't really understand the business. Tune them out."

"That person is never satisfied and is always stirring up trouble of one kind or another. Just ignore them."

If you've ever received—or sent—messages like that, take a moment to think about the implications of these suggestions.

Effective sales leaders don't tune anyone out. True, they don't follow everyone's advice and they don't pretend they have unlimited amounts of time to listen to every problem. But they know that each person's experience and perspective is precious. They don't pretend that people who annoy them or disagree with them are incapable of passing along good ideas.

Bill Gates once said, "Your most unhappy customers are your greatest source of learning." He was absolutely right. He could have added that unhappy salespeople are a great source of learning, too. Be sure to listen for the truth, regardless of the sender. Don't let what other people say about someone—or what you have learned to tell yourself about someone—persuade you that the person does not even deserve a hearing. Their perspective is valid from their point of view. It deserves to be validated, not just tolerated. When someone shares their perspective with you, thank them for doing so—and mean it.

Does this mean no one ever acts like a jerk? That toxic conflicts don't arise? That pointless grudges are never held onto for way too long? Of course not. These things happen. When they do, you have an obligation to deal with them appropriately. But you also have an obligation not to pigeonhole people and not to play favorites.

If a salesperson has a problem or idea to discuss, your team will always be stronger if you can find a way to make sure they feel heard, in particular if they have reason to believe that voices like theirs have been marginalized in the past.

Listen for the truth. Don't pass judgment on the person. Don't assume that someone who was connected to a certain kind of problem in the past will always be connected to that kind of problem. If there has been a conflict or a disagreement or even some hurt feelings, find a way to help the parties step back from that and take a close look at the situation. Ask yourself:

"Even if the way this was said made people uncomfortable, is there a chance that what is being said here is true?"

"How can I confirm that?"

"If it is true, what's the right next step?"

As the leader, you have a responsibility to find a way to continue the dialogue. It's entirely possible that someone sharing feedback with you has been thought of as an outsider or has some history that has led to unfavorability with others in your organization. That doesn't mean they can't point you toward problems that need to be examined. Sometimes, a person's unpopularity is a flashing red light that you should be listening to them. It's possible that others on your team are not approaching issues with an open mind or are unwilling to admit that there is a better way of doing something.

SALES LEADERSHIP KEY 20: IMPLEMENT GOOD IDEAS AND GIVE CREDIT.

If a salesperson who has been tuned out, pigeonholed, or stereotyped in the past comes up with an idea, an insight, or a piece of information that helps your team move forward towards an important goal, make a special point of ensuring they get appropriate credit, in an appropriate forum, for sharing what they shared. Be sure they know you know they made a contribution. This is important for everyone on your team, of course, but it's particularly important when the salesperson who has shared something important has had reason to feel marginalized. You want to look for ways to turn that experience around.

SALES LEADERSHIP KEY 21: KEEP PEOPLE IN THE LOOP.

A big part of respecting someone's truth is keeping them informed about events that impact them. Keep the members of your sales team informed. If they want to know what's happening in a given area that is relevant to their job performance or career growth, look for ways to get them the information they are seeking. Very often, major communication problems arise when there are gaping holes in someone's knowledge base—gaps that are easy to fill and that there is no reason not to fill. When in doubt, lean towards giving people more rather than less information. It's easy for people to feel disrespected when they believe that critical information is being kept from them. Take away that cause for concern if it's within your power to do so.

Here's a common situation where you as the leader will want to find a way to do that. Let's say you have been involved in a major project for months, a project that will affect how sales territories are defined. You've spent a lot of time working on this project and thinking about it. When you talk to the members of the sales team, you assume they know as much about the project's current status as you do. But—they don't! They're still exactly where you left them when you gave them their last update, which was weeks or even months ago. You get frustrated, they get frustrated—everybody loses. How do you keep that kind of problem from happening? By going out of your way to update people constantly about where things stand on projects that affect them.

Do this informally and appropriately, and use any platform you want. Over-communicating about status and progress has little or no downside, assuming that you respect the boundaries between home life and work life and that you keep your communication casual and accessible. Under-communicating, on the other hand, is inevitably going to come back to haunt you.

If you want to harness people's energy and commitment, if you want their full focus and participation, make sure they know they are part of something important. That means keeping them up to date about what is going on. They need to understand where they fit in, what decisions will be affecting them, and how they will need to adjust once those decisions are implemented. When you remember to update them, they feel they are part of the team. When you forget to update them, they don't. People will always work harder for a cause they believe in than they will for something they consider "just a job." They cannot believe in your cause or use their skills and experience to add value to it if they are not in the loop. It's that simple.

Think of this from the employee's perspective. When they don't have information—what do they do? They assume you think their input on that information isn't important. As a result, they feel unappreciated and they lose interest. Yes, as a sales leader, you need to be forward-looking, and that's good. But you also need to slow down, take a look around, and notice when it's time to go back and fill in the blanks for your people so that you have a fully engaged sales team.

SALES LEADERSHIP KEYS: RULE 8

19. Don't prejudge advice based on who gave it.
20. Implement good ideas and give credit.
21. Keep people in the loop.

RULE 9

Build Tomorrow's Leaders

SET PEOPLE UP FOR SUCCESS.

"The delicate balance of mentoring someone is not creating them in your own image, but giving them the opportunity to create themselves."

—STEVEN SPIELBERG

THE ONLY REASON you are reading this book is that I hit the lottery, as it were, in terms of personal career development. I was fortunate enough to have as my coach and mentor one of the truly great business leaders of his era. He challenged me to find ways to pass on what I had learned. If he hadn't, I wouldn't be writing these words.

David Sandler was someone who knew that true leadership was, at its core, all about building good relationships and supporting other people; he was particularly skilled when it came to identifying and supporting emerging sales leaders. I was one of those emerging sales leaders, and a day doesn't go by that I don't try to live up to his standard. What follows are four critical best practices I picked up from Sandler about a key concern for anyone who hopes to lead a team to the kind of success that is scalable and that endures: building the next generation of leaders.

SALES LEADERSHIP KEY 22: MAKE IT ALL ABOUT THEM.

The phrase "servant leadership" wasn't as popular as it is now when David Sandler hired me, but it captures his working philosophy perfectly. Sandler was not about domination or head games. He was there to help me get where I needed to go. He made this abundantly clear on multiple occasions, and there was no artifice or pretense or manipulation to this kind of communication when he shared it with me. He was serious. He was committed to helping me become a better leader and a better person, and I knew it.

Do each of the people on your sales team know that you are personally committed to helping them grow and develop, both personally and professionally? How do they know that?

SALES LEADERSHIP KEY 23: SET UP GUARDRAILS AND TIMELINES.

Sander was a master of a skill that today we share and role-play extensively in our management programs: setting up guardrails.

These are clear guidelines that, within certain predetermined, mutually agreed-upon parameters, allow the salesperson reporting to you to make their own decisions and—this is crucial—to fail.

Notice how different this is from setting no clear limits then shifting instantly into Critical Parent mode when something goes wrong. Sandler knew that failing and learning from failure is how adults learn. He built that knowledge into his mentoring process. As his mentee, I knew that as long as I stayed within the guardrails, there would be no repercussions for trial-and-error in our relationship. I felt safe. I knew the things that I could decide. I knew the amount of money that I could spend. I knew the names of the people I should be involving when I was making decisions in certain areas.

Sandler was also great when it came to setting deadlines. He didn't just tell me when he wanted something finished. He set up check-in points along the way, so we could both take a close look at how the project was coming. I learned quickly that it was a great idea, during our meetings, to be able to point to incremental progress that supported the completion date we had both agreed to. This was an extension of the guardrail concept. As long as I kept making verifiable progress toward the agreed-upon date (or spoke up and communicated with Sandler if I saw there was going to be a problem), he and I were OK. He also set benchmarks that gave me enough time to pivot if I needed to.

Since then, not only have I built the Sandler business around these concepts for developing teams and leaders, I've built them into our management program. The whole reason this approach works as well as it does connects to something we call the "two P's": permission and protection. David Sandler gave me permission to make decisions, to try different things, to experiment, and he could protect me as long as two conditions were fulfilled: I stayed within the guardrails we determined, and I personally believed that what I was doing was a good idea.

Sandler realized, and I realized, that what I decided might not always deliver a great result, but I had his permission to do it as long as I stayed within the lines and I was able to tell him why I thought what I had done was a good idea. As long as I came through on those two fronts, I had permission to do what I wanted. When things did go wrong—which of course sometimes they did—he never played the game of finding someone to blame and pointing fingers. He protected me (and others), because he knew that the blame game causes people not to stretch—and when they don't stretch, they don't learn.

SALES LEADERSHIP KEY 24: DELEGATE EFFECTIVELY.

Delegation is a crucial leadership skill. If you do not master it, your team will not be able to scale its success. Period.

Some sales leaders delegate only when there's something on

their plate that they don't feel like doing; or, they don't have time to do; or, they are not even certain they can do. Then, as they're delegating, they don't bother to explain what success is supposed to look like to the person assigned the task. David Sandler never pulled people into that trap. When he delegated something to me, he made sure both he and I had a very clear sense of what the desired outcome was. He didn't delude himself into thinking, "Mattson is smart; he knows what I want." He knew that, very often, direct reports don't know specifically what their leaders want. Even if he thought I knew what the deliverable was, he would take a few minutes so go over it with me so we could make sure we were each on the same page.

What's more—and this is crucial—he didn't delegate things based on what he wanted to get off his plate. He made a point of delegating tasks to me based on what he knew would help me learn, grow, and develop so I could gain experience and get ready for my next role. Of course, that meant he and I both had to have a clear idea of my personal development path. We had discussions about that, as well. This is an essential part of the delegation picture, one that too many leaders ignore. Ask yourself if what you're assigning a person to do is helping them learn and grow. If so, how? What do they need to experience next to move to the next level of their development? How can you help them get there?

71% of Fortune 500 companies have formal mentorship programs.[10]

SALES LEADERSHIP KEY 25: HAVE BOTH A PRE-STRATEGY MEETING AND A DEBRIEF.

Feedback is important, yes. Sandler and I had plenty of "post-mortem" discussions in which we discussed how a given project I was in charge of had gone. But we also had plenty of planning discussions so we could talk about strategy. These were typically part of the one-on-one coaching process. He would ask me: "What do you plan on doing with such-and-such a project? Why that? What other approaches did you consider? Why did you discount them?" That kind of discussion is just as important as the debrief—perhaps even more important—because it helps people get their head around what they should and shouldn't be doing.

Many sales leaders fall into the habit of focusing entirely on the post-mortem: "Let's talk about what you did." If you want to support salespeople fully, though, you will also want to have some discussions about what they are planning to do, and why. In pre-strategy meetings, you can use gentle questioning to shine a light on areas where the person hasn't yet had a lot of experience. Sandler would ask me questions such as, "Why did you pick that approach? What will you need to make that work? What happens if...?" and so on. It was like a grandmaster teaching a young chess player how to think three or four or five moves ahead.

Many sales leaders skip the pre-strategy session entirely. I believe that's a mistake. You want to focus your efforts on the important pre-game questions, as well as on the post-game analysis.

I think of the pre-strategy talk as parallel to a discussion I might have with one of my kids about a big test at school. If I have only one option, I would rather help my child prepare for the test and execute on it well than go over all the wrong answers after the fact. Before the test, if you work with them, you still have the chance to influence the outcome.

SALES LEADERSHIP KEYS: RULE 9

22. Make it all about them.
23. Set up guardrails and timelines.
24. Delegate effectively.
25. Have both a pre-strategy meeting and a debrief.

RULE 10

Make Accountability the Norm

CREATE A CULTURE OF ACCOUNTABILITY.

"At the end of the day we are accountable to ourselves. Our success is the result of what we do."

—Catherine Pulsifer

PERHAPS IT'S HUMAN nature, but many sales teams struggle with accountability. How can you ensure that your salespeople will hold themselves accountable, day after day, week after week, month after month?

Of course you want people to do what they say they are going to do. Yet often sales teams spend inordinate amounts of time and energy trying to make sure this actually happens.

Your challenge as a leader is to make accountability the default setting, the norm—the way you do business in your team. With that goal in mind, here are two powerful strategies I would suggest you take a look at.

82% of executives surveyed by the Landmark Workplace Accountability Study reported major challenges with accountability in their organization.[11]

SALES LEADERSHIP KEY 26: HOLD YOURSELF ACCOUNTABLE FIRST.

The simple definition of accountability is following through on what you say you're going to do and holding yourself responsible if you don't. Organizational culture has a huge impact on whether that happens. If you've got a workplace culture where people routinely are not doing what they've told you they're going to do, that isn't just a problem with the individual team members—that's also a problem with leadership. Team members are picking that habit up from someone—their sales leader. You can't tell your kids not to smoke as you're going through your second pack at dinner. It doesn't work. They'll say, "Why should I quit smoking cigarettes? Look at you!" Your actions have to be congruent with your words.

Accountability must begin with the leader. It must begin with looking in the mirror and asking yourself some tough questions:

"Am I setting clear expectations about what I will deliver and when, and then following through in the way that I expect others to follow through?"

"Am I being congruent? Am I doing everything I say I'm going to do?"

"Am I keeping my word?"

"If there's an obstacle to being able to keep my word, do I raise that issue myself with the people who are counting on me, openly deal with the situation, and detail my plan for resolving it?"

It can be easy to sell yourself on the idea that lack of accountability is a problem with the people on your team, or with your hiring process, or with something else that's not the face staring back at you in the mirror in the morning. But the reality is that a lack of accountability on a sales team is almost always a symptom of something else that's happening—something to do with the sales leader's decisions and interactions.

Salespeople listen to what you say, but they also watch what you do. If someone on your team isn't doing what they say they are going to do or is not doing it the way you want it done, whose issue is that? You may want to believe that it's entirely their issue—but is it?

Most leaders don't realize when there is a cancer in their organization called "a sense of entitlement": thinking and acting as if the rules and the behavioral norms are in place for people other than yourself. This cancer can destroy any organization. It typically spreads under cover of being a supportive leader.

Yes, people need to be held accountable. But that needs to happen in the right sequence. The critical question is not whether you're going to hold people accountable. It's who you're going to hold accountable first.

If you are serious about building and sustaining an accountable working culture, it always needs to be first an issue you are committed to for yourself, on a personal level. There is only one way your people will start buying into, supporting, and defending a workplace culture where people can count on each other, and that is to experience you as the leader doing what you say you're going to do, day in and day out.

When you say you want an accountable team, what you're really saying is that you want a team where everyone can rely on everyone else performing the job they have taken on the responsibility of doing. You can make that kind of team happen—but only if you hold yourself accountable and set the best example possible.

SALES LEADERSHIP KEY 27: TAKE FULL PERSONAL RESPONSIBILITY.

Picture the perfect military leader. It doesn't matter whether the person you have in your mind is based on your own experience in the service, or on some period of history that you've studied, or on some movie or television show you've watched. Just form, in your own mind, the image of a truly great commanding officer. Got it?

Now. Here's a question. What happens when something goes wrong in the field, and that officer gets called on the carpet for the mistake or failure by their superior?

I'll tell you what happens. That officer takes full responsibility for whatever happened. They are accountable, even if they had no idea that it had gone wrong until everyone else found out there was an issue. I can remember scenes like when I was a kid, watching World War II movies. I'd think to myself, "Wait a minute. Why is that officer taking the blame? He didn't do anything."

I was wrong. That officer did do something, something very important. He accepted a leadership position. That means he accepted personal responsibility for the performance of the team, in addition to responsibility for his own actions and choices.

Salespeople notice when their leaders fail to step up and own a problem. Not only do they notice, they remember it for a long, long time. Years before I met David Sandler, I got an unforgettable lesson in just what such a lack of leadership looks like.

This was my very first sales job, and it was before we had any cool software that would help us price deals out accurately using pro forma calculations. We figured out pricing by scribbling down numbers and hoping we got everything right. Once, my boss and I came up with the pricing for a certain deal together. What we didn't realize was that we had screwed up the margins. We thought the margin on the deal was low but acceptable. It turned out that the company would actually lose money on the deal.

When the owner of the company found out about this, he was not happy. He called both me and my boss into his office—and went into attack mode. But here's the thing: The owner focused all of his anger at me, presumably because I was the youngest person in the room and it was easier to yell at me.

Somehow the fact that my boss had led the pricing process never entered the conversation. Everything was about me. The owner wanted to know: How could I have made such a stupid mistake? Didn't I understand that I had cost the company a lot of money? What was I going to do to fix the problem? My boss sat there and watched me taking on incoming fire without ever coming to my defense or mentioning the fact that he had helped me come up with the pricing. It would have been a painful and disorienting experience for anyone, but it was particularly difficult for a young salesperson just getting started in his career.

Afterwards, I asked my boss why he hadn't spoken up on my behalf. He wouldn't meet my eye. He seemed to think he had done me some kind of favor by suggesting to the owner that he keep the meeting short. He also mumbled something about the importance of letting the owner rant in those situations, because "responding only makes it worse."

I knew I had been unfairly blamed for something that he and I had jointly worked on, something that he should have been responsible for, because, let's face it, he was the boss and I had just joined the company. But my boss would not admit any of that—or even talk about it.

I decided I could never trust him again. Don't let your salespeople come to the same conclusion about you.

SALES LEADERSHIP KEY 28: USE RACI.

Has this ever happened at your company? One person steps up and takes on an important project, completes it, and then discovers that an important but undiscussed issue was overlooked. As a result, a lot of the work has to be done all over again.

Or this? Team A completes an important project, only to learn that Team B has important insights and opinions to share and never got the chance to do so. Not only are there problems with the project, but now there is a morale problem.

Or this? Everyone imagines a certain important task is being done by "someone"—but in fact no one has taken on this task. It gets skipped, and people start pointing fingers, wasting everyone's time and energy.

The RACI system is a critical best practice we share with our leadership coaching clients who want to address these kinds of problems and improve personal, team, and organizational accountability. RACI is a tool for clarifying exactly who's doing what on any given initiative. It's invaluable for those who want a culture of accountability, and it's particularly important in enterprise-selling situations where there are teams from multiple departments involved in pursuing an opportunity. If you're not already using RACI to keep track of the roles on a project, let me urge you to start doing so immediately. Clarity on roles and responsibilities is essential when it comes to accountability, and that is exactly what this tool delivers.

RACI stands for responsible, accountable, consulted, informed. These four simple labels drive this time-tested process for assigning responsibility at the right levels to all participants in an enterprise selling initiative—or any initiative. Assign one of those four tags to each team member taking part in the project.

Responsible individuals are those actively involved in implementing and managing the initiative. The list of responsible individuals can extend all the way down to the front lines of the organization. It's theoretically possible, but not likely, that the responsible person in a given initiative will be you, the leader. (If you are always responsible for executing hands-on tasks, your delegation skills need work.) People who are responsible for something must know that they are responsible for it—and they must know when and how they will be expected to fulfill their responsibility. If you find yourself in the responsible role, be sure to follow through on all of your commitments. Otherwise you will lack congruence when you ask others to follow through on theirs.

The **accountable** individual is the one person who is ultimately answerable for the completion of the task. This person also delegates to those in other categories. Let's assume that's you. Ultimately, it is the leader who is personally accountable for the success or failure of every initiative the team takes on. Responsible and accountable parties must agree on all the key deliverables, on the resources available for completing them, and on the communication schedule. Save yourself stress and disappointment by spending some time up front clarifying the who, what, why, when, and how.

People who are **consulted** are involved in the planning, implementation, and management stages as resources because they possess expertise or offer important perspectives (such as firsthand experience with customers who will be affected by the project). These individuals could be senior company leaders, members of your board, or trusted advisors you rely on for guidance.

Someone who is **informed** doesn't have any involvement

other than receiving information about your project and its progress. They may need to do something important once the project is complete, such as update the inventory figures when a shipment arrives. Typically, communication with these people is only in one direction, but they're free to weigh in at any time.

RACI is a responsibility identification process that creates clarity about who is doing what and when. It is the bedrock of team accountability. Use it!

SALES LEADERSHIP KEYS: RULE 10

26. Hold yourself accountable first.
27. Take full personal responsibility.
28. Use RACI.

RULE 11

Create Team Ownership of Ideas and Solutions

LEVERAGE THE WISDOM AND CREATIVITY OF THE TEAM; GIVE OTHERS THE CREDIT.

"Remember, teamwork begins by building trust. And the only way to do that is to overcome our need for invulnerability."

—Patrick Lencioni

TEAM OWNERSHIP OF IDEAS is, for many teams, the great untapped resource of sales leadership. America's thirty-third president, Harry S. Truman, may have captured the force of this concept best when he said, "It is amazing what you can accomplish if you do not care who gets the credit." I would add only one asterisk to clarify Truman's famous observation: You have to not only not care if you get the credit but you also have to be vulnerable enough to ask for help in generating or implementing the initiative. If both of those conditions are in place, there is indeed no limit on what your team and your organization can accomplish.

Let me share the precise moment when I realized this core leadership truth. Years ago, I had a bad habit of taking on too much and trying to solve every problem myself. (This is a problem many who lead sales teams struggle with.) During one of our coaching sessions, David Sandler (who had dropped hints about this issue several times before) asked me, "How many years of experience in business do you have, Dave?"

Proudly, I said, "Ten."

"And how many years of experience does your team have collectively?"

I did a quick and dirty calculation involving the experience of the 12 people who reported to me, and then said, "240."

He nodded and then stared at the ceiling thoughtfully, as though he were considering an intricate math problem. I knew that when Sandler did this, it meant a lesson of some kind was on the way. He didn't disappoint.

"So are you saying," he asked, "that you would rather solve this problem with ten years of experience than with 240 years of experience?"

I didn't have to answer. The lesson was clear.

In this chapter, we look at two situations where team brainpower and team ownership of ideas and solutions can make all the difference: 1) the situation where you have not yet made up your mind (covered in Sales Leadership Key 29), and 2) the situation where you have made up your mind and you want to be sure people are on board with the new direction (covered in Sales Leadership Key 30). It is important to notice, before you look at the tactics I will be sharing here, that both of these situations require you to take off your superhero cape and ask people for help. There is a paradox at work here: Pretending that you never, ever need to ask for help is actually the ultimate position of weakness as a leader; being willing to admit vulnerability by saying out loud that you do want and need help from your team is the ultimate position of strength.

SALES LEADERSHIP KEY 29: CALL THE TEAM TOGETHER FOR A TEAM STORM SESSION.

You hired great people. There is a lot of talent on your payroll. Why not use it? Put the team's combined brainpower to work on a major challenge you face. Get them all in the same (physical or digital) room and get a special kind of discussion going—the kind of discussion that makes disagreement a positive cultural event, an opportunity for everyone to speak their mind frankly and express themselves so that you get the chance to evaluate all sides of an issue. Then, guide the group gently back into a team-first mindset.

We call this special discussion a Team Storm (as in brainstorm) session. Like the RACI system, it is especially useful in team selling and enterprise sales situations. It is designed to create a safe space in which everyone is thinking creatively and contributing. Think about how many times brainstorming sessions in the past have allowed only a couple of people to dominate the proceedings. Who knows how many good ideas go unexpressed in that kind of session? That is the opposite of what you're going for here. Remember, some people on your team are going to be less inclined to speak up in public than others. (Steady Relators, in particular, often need a little encouragement.) You can use this tool and the power of team engagement to help everyone feel comfortable making a contribution and to build a sense of belonging and team cohesion.

When asked what the most important reason for staying at their current company is, 37% of respondents surveyed by Gusto identified "working with a great team" as the primary factor.[12]

This Team Storm meeting is extremely powerful both as a problem-solving tool and as a cultural statement. In it, everyone expresses their individual views respectfully but without apology and then unites behind a single course of action, as a team. Because you're the leader, you may either choose to facilitate this session or delegate that task to someone else.

The Team Storm process has five steps, outlined below.

Step 1: Problem statement. This is the initial statement of the opportunity, the challenge, or the problem you are asking the group to help you with. It is delivered in a simple, clear headline, not in a rambling format.

The problem statement is delivered via action orientation, preceded by the words "how to." For example, if the problem that you're concerned about is how to make quota with four weeks left in the quarter, the problem statement is not going to be, "Making up for lousy projections." It's going to be "How to generate X amount of revenue by the 30th of this month." It's important to lead the problem statement with the words "how to" because this promotes a positive mindset that the *how* is discernible and waiting to be acted on.

Step 2: Background. This involves providing the information and clarifications that might be needed to understand the problem. If your team members are already invested in finding a solution to the problem, this need not be a lengthy part of the session. Provide a quick context check, get everybody on the same page, and move on.

Step 3: Idea generation. This is the heart of the Team Storm. Hands go up, ideas are shared, contrasting ideas are offered, and there is vigorous discussion. This is how the problem statement is addressed. Make sure all the ideas are recorded faithfully. If everyone is in the same room, the ideas can go up on flip-chart sheets, which can then cover the walls. If this is a digital meeting, task someone with capturing everything and sharing it in a format that all participants can see and comment on.

Bear in mind that Step 3 is all about active engagement. This is where you look for creative thinking. Encourage people to avoid investing too much time deconstructing other people's ideas in this step. If they think a certain approach won't work, they should say so briefly and directly and then propose a measure of their own that they believe will work. The key is to get a lot of ideas out there, as quickly as possible.

The facilitator will close out Step 3 with a process called the *combination of ideas*. What does that mean? It involves taking ideas that are very similar and combining them, with the concurrence of the people who came up with the ideas. Why do you do this? Well, since you are about to move forward to a voting process, combining similar ideas ensures the maximum value of the votes. Otherwise, people would scatter votes and make consensus more difficult by choosing similar ideas.

Step 4: Idea selection. This is where the team votes on the list of ideas as they have been formulated and consolidated by the facilitator. The team closes ranks on one solution that they will recommend to you, the leader. If there's an idea that you as the leader can't get your arms around or don't think is viable, this is the time to say so. You have the chance to veto any option the team comes up with, but I would urge you to use that power sparingly. If you ask the team to come up with an idea in response to a pressing problem, it's a good plan to keep an open mind and look for ways to stand behind the best idea that they deliver.

Step 5: Action plan/next steps. The facilitator now leads a conclusive discussion of who's going to do what and when, in support of the solution chosen. Use the RACI system outlined in Rule 10. The stronger and more time-driven the commitments are in Team Storm Step 5, the better the chance of success in resolving the problem.

That's Team Storm. It can transform your team and deliver extraordinary outcomes with lightning speed. That's the key to its success: speed. This is a rapid group brainstorming exercise that drives engagement and team buy-in. Use it to generate a storm of ideas—and then narrow those down to the very best option.

What about those situations where you know what you want to do, and you are eager to make sure the initiative is seen as a "we-first" idea, rather than a "me-first" idea? Read on.

SALES LEADERSHIP KEY 30: MAKE THE TEAM PART OF THE CHANGE.

Not many people like change, unless they cause it. When they are the cause of change, they call it "innovation"—and then they love it. It's funny how that works.

When a major change like a relocation or a revision to the sales team's compensation plan comes along, it's understandable that team members are going to be wary or resistant at first. People want to feel like an active participant in the big events in their lives, as opposed to being a victim of a change they have no control over. That's only natural.

Great sales leaders take advantage of this fact, rather than fighting it. They follow three critical steps to build that all-important team buy-in on critical initiatives that need to happen but that haven't yet won wide support within the team.

Step 1. Announce it early—and make the discussion about how. Lay the groundwork early by sharing what you have in mind, explaining why you made the decision you did, encouraging questions, and getting people's feedback. Give yourself and the team as much time as possible to process the new situation. Don't make the mistake of simply announcing the new rules and then vanishing, without preparing people for the change.

If a big new change that affects everyone is taking place in January, take the time to create and follow a well-thought-out change plan well in advance of that date—one that includes lots of communication with the team. If it's a particularly important change, I recommend you start your messaging several months in advance: October, say. Give yourself plenty of time to gather feedback and suggestions from all of those who will be affected by the change you have in mind. The members of your team must feel they've had input on what will happen in January. Give them the opportunity to share that input. The goal here is not to allow your team to make your decisions, but to start the conversation and to eliminate the possibility of someone kicking up in January by saying, "Hey, this came out of nowhere."

Very early on, you will want to draw a clear line between the *what* and the *how*. As you hold your preliminary discussions with the team, make it clear that you're not looking for feedback on whether the change will take place—it will—but you are looking for help on how it will unfold.* Let your people know that while the *what* isn't up for discussion, you are deeply interested in their thoughts on the very best ways for the team to get where it is headed. Be sure you listen actively to what they share with you. Celebrate and circulate those positive suggestions you hear that cover how best to implement the upcoming change.

* You may decide that it makes sense to use the Team Storm process when you are looking for input on some minor aspect of the *what*, but make sure it's clear that the biggest strokes of the change initiative you are implementing are not up for negotiation.

This is what changes the initiative from a "me-first" idea to a "we-first" idea.

Step 2: Identify the champions of change. As you talk to your team about the approaching change, you will notice that some people are more receptive to adapting than others. Your job as a leader is to spot those team members who are the most eager to help you make the new system work and then create opportunities for them to share with the team what they're doing to prepare. These people will be your champions of change. For instance: If you're changing the compensation plan to better reward major account acquisition, you'll want to identify the salespeople who are eager to change their prospecting and relationship-building activities to support that new goal. You'll also want to give them a chance to share with the rest of the team, firsthand, what they plan to do to succeed using the new plan. After the rollout begins, any relevant success stories your champions can share with the team will be important, too. Yes, you have the formal title of leader, but the title only does so much. It is the alliances you forge and reinforce that will make your life easier as you implement this change initiative.

Step 3: Communicate regularly about the upcoming change, using multiple channels. The key words here are "regularly" and "multiple channels." This is the part some sales leaders forget.

When I work with clients, I often hear this: "I don't know how people could possibly be confused. After all, I sent out a memo!" Or: "We talked about this!" Sending out a single memo or talking about the issue at a couple of meetings is not enough. People process information in different ways, so important messaging must be repeated if it's going to have an impact. That means a single email won't do the trick when it comes to getting your team on board for major change. A single team meeting won't do it, either. If some of your people work exclusively off-site—an arrangement becoming more and more common—a single video or a single webinar won't be enough to win team buy-in, either.

In preparation for the big transition you plan to implement, you will want to use all available communication channels—any that are appropriate to your working environment. By creating an effective drip campaign about what's going to be different next year, you'll keep this subject on your team's collective radar screen. A week should not go by without the team getting some kind of positive messaging about the upcoming change. Your core message doesn't have to be long—in fact, concise is probably best—but it does need to repeat over time. Take full advantage of multiple communication platforms as you share true stories from the champions of change on the front lines. Think in terms of a wave of communication, not a single discussion. That wave should constantly send and reinforce the key messages: 1) This is what's happening; 2) This is why it's happening; and 3) Here's a success story that shows what it looks like in action.

Remember: You may be thinking about this issue all the time, but the members of your team are only likely to think about it when they are reminded of it. People are people. They get distracted, and they need reminding. That doesn't mean your communications aren't important, it just means you have multiple chances to ensure the message actually registers with your team. Use those chances to your advantage.

SALES LEADERSHIP KEYS: RULE 11

29. Call the team together for a Team Storm session.
30. Make the team part of the change.

RULE 12

Don't Wimp Out

SET PRIORITIES THAT PUSH YOU BEYOND YOUR COMFORT ZONE.

"You may encounter many defeats, but you must not be defeated."

—Maya Angelou

CONSIDER THIS SCENARIO. You have made a personal commitment to get in better physical shape. Part of that commitment is a schedule you have set for yourself to get up early three days a week—Monday, Wednesday, and Friday—and jog for a mile and a half before getting ready for work. The first Monday rolls around. The alarm goes off. You stare at it. It's the moment of truth. Will you get out of your warm, comfortable bed and head out into the cold morning to keep your commitment?

Or will you wimp out?

Wimping out means choosing not to align your actions

with your goals, not to stretch, not to push yourself, not to go beyond your comfort zone. This choice carries major cultural consequences. As the leader, you set the example for everyone else in the organization when it comes to stepping out of your own comfort zone. If you consistently choose to play it safe and stay within that comfort zone, the salespeople around you are, sooner or later, going to notice that. Make no mistake, once they do, they will follow your example.*

On the other hand, if you make a habit of moving beyond what you are presently comfortable and familiar with because you know that busting out of comfort zones means learning more, achieving more, and coming closer to the goal of fulfilling your own potential, then your salespeople will notice that behavior and will start to emulate it. As the leader, you set the tone. Your team can either get used to wimping out and holding on as tightly as possible to the status quo, or they can get used to pushing themselves past their previous levels of performance and establishing a new standard for their personal best. It's up to you. Your decision about whether to wimp out plays a huge role in determining whether others on the

* By the way, I'm not saying never to cut yourself any slack. I'm just saying to be aware of the times when your choice to go beyond your own comfort zone can set a good example for the team. This whole subject, of course, is situational. If you are on vacation and you decide it makes sense to sleep in, more power to you.

team will follow suit and whether you will accept wimp-out approaches from others.

Here are two powerful strategies that will help you strengthen the habit of moving beyond your personal comfort zone.

SALES LEADERSHIP KEY 31: DO THE MOST UNCOMFORTABLE THING FIRST.

David Sandler had a saying: "You only have to be courageous for five minutes at a time." There are always going to be parts of your job that make you feel uncomfortable—for instance, an interaction you are not looking forward to about CRM compliance with a tech-averse veteran salesperson. When you set up your daily to-do list, you want to put that item first. The longer you put it off, the more you will find yourself thinking about how difficult the discussion is going to be and the less effective you eventually will be when you finally do have the conversation.

Don't wimp out. Don't let the action you are avoiding own you. If you know, deep down, that you need to do something unpleasant, do it as soon as possible. Not only will this make your whole day easier and liberate you every time you do it, it will set a far better standard for your team to follow. You don't want them putting off important next steps just because they are feeling a little discomfort. Show them how it's done.

SALES LEADERSHIP KEY 32: TELL PEOPLE YOUR MOST IMPORTANT GOALS.

Put some social pressure on yourself. When you take on a goal that you know is likely to take you beyond your comfort zone, share what you plan to do with other people whose opinion matters to you. This makes it a little harder for you to crawl back under the covers when the alarm goes off.

If you make a commitment at home that your spouse knows about, you're going to be more motivated to align your actions with the words you've spoken out loud. This principle applies to both workplace and personal goals. When you decide you want to make a change in your personal life, share that goal with those that the change will most affect who will be motivated to support you. When you decide you want to make a change in your business, share that goal with those in your business that the change will affect most and who will be best positioned to help you turn the goal into reality. Tell them you want to get out of your comfort zone—and mean it.

Once, someone on our team was struggling. During a coaching session we suggested that she write down her goals and post them in a spot where her family could see them all the time. You can guess what happened—the family members started asking about what kind of progress she was making on her goals, and she stepped up her game. She reached a point where she would take action in anticipation of the questions because she didn't want to give her family bad news. That strategy worked. She had a major turnaround.

According to a study conducted by Dr. Gail Matthews at the Dominican University in California, participants were 42% more likely to achieve goals when they wrote them down.[13]

SALES LEADERSHIP KEY 33: WHEN YOU GET CLOSE TO ACHIEVING A GOAL, UP THE GOAL.

This is something David Sandler, acting as my coach when I was a salesperson, always encouraged me to do. If my income goal was X and I was on track to meet that goal, typically about 70% of the way there he would encourage me to set a new, higher goal of Y. He knew that setting the new goal and connecting it to something that was truly important to me would energize me and keep me from falling into a pattern of coasting. Have the same kind of discussion with your salespeople—and, yes, from time to time, with yourself.

Coasting is wimping out. Don't let coasting become your pattern or the pattern of the salespeople who report to you. Don't let coasting become what you demonstrate to the team or to the rest of the organization as the way you do business. Don't let coasting become the acceptable standard of behavior. When you are almost at the point where you've reached your goal, you tend to think you will hit it. That means moving it is no big deal. It's the perfect time to raise the stakes.

You have more control over what you can achieve than you imagine—and so does the salesperson who reports to you. You can each set the stretch goal a little further beyond what you once believed you were capable of. Think about this as being like going to the gym and lifting weights. Let's suppose your goal is to do 12 reps. Right about the time you hit 10 reps, your mind starts sending you a message: "This is hard!" But what happens? You keep on pushing. In fact, you push past that message and you hit the goal. Here's the interesting thing, though. If you had set the goal at 15 reps, you wouldn't have gotten that message until you hit, say, 13 reps. You can push past that, too! You really can make your goals more aggressive if you want. It's all a matter of picking the right moment and understanding how your own mind works.

SALES LEADERSHIP KEYS: RULE 12

31. Do the most uncomfortable thing first.
32. Tell people your most important goals.
33. When you get close to achieving a goal, up the goal.

RULE 13

Develop the Right Processes and the Tools That Support Them

CREATE AND IMPLEMENT PLAYBOOKS.

"One accurate measurement is worth a thousand expert opinions."

—GRACE HOPPER

PROCESS GETS A BAD RAP. To most people, hearing the word "process" in relation to what they do in the workplace instantly summons up another word, one that nobody enjoys experiencing firsthand—"micromanagement." I'm not entirely sure why people have made this connection so consistently, but I am sure that process (properly understood and properly implemented) is the exact opposite of micromanagement. Let me share a little story—about you!—that will illustrate what I mean by this.

Once upon a time, you decided to buy a vacation home. This was a nice little getaway right next to a lake that you and your family used for long weekends, holidays, family get-togethers, you name it. There was a speedboat you could use if the weather was warm. And a dock. And a campfire. It was a great place for just relaxing, and you and your family always had a great time there.

Then came the day that your oldest son went off to college. A couple of months later, he asked if he and his roommate could spend a long weekend at the vacation house. You had no problem with this in principle, but you wondered: Would the place be locked up properly? Would the speedboat be stowed in the right spot at the dock? Would the campfire be cleared of any food waste that might attract animals? Would the garbage be bagged up and placed in the bins for collection, and would the bins be closed securely? Since you were not planning to visit the property for several months, these were pretty important questions.

Instead of saying no or giving your son a long lecture about all the things he needed to do, you did something better than either of those options. You wrote up a checklist. Basically, it looked like this.

1. Here's what to do when you get to the house.

2. Here's who to call in an emergency.

3. Here's what to do when you are getting ready to leave.

You also provided a concise written overview of all the stuff your son was likely to need.

1. Here is where to find the keys to the speedboat and where they should go when you're done.
2. Here is where to find garbage bags.
3. Here is where to find firewood.

The whole thing was less than a page long, but it covered everything that needed to happen. You texted it to your son, who stored it right on his phone and used it. Your son and his roommate had a great time. Everything got taken care of that needed to get taken care of. The next time you showed up at the vacation house, you saw for yourself that there had been no problems.

Now, is that checklist micromanagement? I don't think so. I think of it more as liberation for everyone involved. Your son knew exactly what to do and where to find everything that would be needed, and you knew that you didn't have to worry about anything being overlooked. Those are exactly the outcomes that a good process delivers. They are the outcomes that the best leaders commit themselves to whenever they talk about process. Process simply identifies what the steps to success are.

Process tells your people exactly what they need to do (or avoid doing). It's an essential part of the guardrails discussion I mentioned in Rule 9. Why wouldn't you want to document the essential steps, the best practices, the available tools, and the most common mistakes, as well as the best ways to avoid them? This makes it incredibly easy for your team to operate within the guardrails you identify, move as quickly or as slowly as they need to in order to hit the mark for you, and learn as they go along, picking up momentum, and delivering a successful outcome for you, over and over and over again.

By the way, what you call your process matters a great deal when it comes to getting people to follow it. Start talking about the steps of a process, and people's eyes tend to glaze over. Call the same steps a checklist or a playbook, and people lean into what you're saying. This is because these kinds of names tap into the basic human desire to follow success. At heart, people really do want to use the proven model, the most efficient way to do something. No one wants to reinvent the wheel.

In this chapter, you learn how to get the right checklists and tools into your people's hands so that you feel so comfortable you don't have to even think about micromanaging anyone. (For more on avoiding micromanagement, see Rule 14.)

SALES LEADERSHIP KEY 34: DOCUMENT BEST PRACTICES INTO A PLAYBOOK.

Have you ever watched a sports team—a football team, say—and been so struck by the team's precision, its effectiveness, and its certainty about who's doing what and when that you thought to yourself, "Wow! That is one incredibly talented team"?

I know I have. And yes, that team must have talent. But what the fans don't see as they're watching the team execute on the field is all that happens behind the scenes to make that great team and the individual performances possible. Specifically, they don't see the creation of the team's playbook.

That's a really critical piece of the puzzle. It's something every professional team spends a lot of time on, even though the fans aren't watching. When a new player arrives on the team, what's the first thing they have to do? Learn the team's playbook! Without a viable playbook, the quarterback might just step up, take a position, call out a play, and see the entire team look up in total confusion, each with an expression that translates roughly as, "What are you talking about?"

The football team's playbook is the compilation of the rigorously vetted best practices that will be implemented during the game. It's the product of a lot of discussion, a lot of research, and a lot of important internal decisions about what works and what doesn't. It draws on player experiences, coaching experiences, and the shared experiences of both players and coaches—in practice and during games. I'm talking about U.S. football because I'm American, but the same principle applies to rugby or soccer or basketball or any other team sport you want.

Of course, this operating principle is not limited to the world of sports. Pilots may have decades of experience, but they still go through a checklist each time they fly. Surgeons have an established sequence of doing things—a list of tasks that need to be done in the right order for the procedure to succeed, even if the doctor has performed the procedure a thousand times. The point is, continuous improvement requires a playbook, and your team's playbook should be just as carefully thought out, just as carefully documented, just as carefully studied and practiced, and just as frequently updated as that of other professionals. You need to bring your salespeople through the same kind of process.

The takeaway here is both simple and far-reaching: Create and circulate a documented playbook of best practices for anything and everything that occurs with your team on an ongoing basis.

- **Create a playbook for yourself.** A sales leader's playbook may include things like weekly check-ins with salespeople, coaching sessions, quarterly business reviews with major clients, and team meetings.

- **Create playbooks for your team.** A salesperson's playbook is likely to include things like prospecting activity, relationship building, qualifying prospects, professional development, territory development, account management, and networking, referral, and business-introduction behaviors.

Bottom line: Create clearly documented, tested, step-by-step processes for more consistent outcomes, and make sure your people know you expect them to follow those processes.

Your playbook is your operating system. It should be a shared collection of action items, talk-tracks, and best practices that enable your whole team to stay on the same page, deliver predictable outcomes, and operate at the highest possible level of efficiency. It should be a written document, not an "I'll know it when I see it" mental list of priorities. That last point is vitally important. Winging it doesn't win games—or championships. For both a sports team and the sales team, a good playbook is the opposite of winging it.

Great processes are not static. They are subject to scheduled reviews and updates. Processes that become outdated become unused, and that's exactly what you do not want. It's a good idea to review individual playbooks as necessary during coaching sessions and to set up an annual audit of the various processes your team follows as a group. Each review can be a Team Storm session led by someone who uses the process in question regularly, and each should result in a revised, dated document with the very latest best practices—a document that all the other members of the team feel good about using. That way, it's a "we-first" playbook, something everybody helped to create and everyone can use to execute the things that are most important for them to do. Thanks to the annual schedule, your organization is not then bogged down by constant process review.

Process improvements in manufacturing enabled 3M to save roughly $30 million per year by redesigning, reusing, or recycling waste materials.[14]

SALES LEADERSHIP KEY 35: CHOOSE TECHNOLOGY FROM AN ORGANIZATIONAL PERSPECTIVE.

A common trap that sales team fall into is that of letting salespeople choose their own favorite technology tools. You end up with competing prospect management systems, competing archiving systems, competing video conferencing tools, and so on. I personally saw a situation where one company was paying for five different services to manage and archive its data. This is confusing for everyone.

The best way to avoid this kind of situation is for the sales leader to do a tools inventory on an annual basis. Make it clear to everyone that tool acquisition and use is a strategic issue, not a matter of individual preference. In each major functional category—prospect tracking, account management, productivity, conferencing, whatever—there needs to be one designated provider and one playbook for people to learn and follow when using the tool in question. That way there is a common language and process you can update and revise over time, as needed. Everyone can understand the technology and how to use it, regardless of the role they're playing in the organization.

SALES LEADERSHIP KEYS: RULE 13

34. Document best practices into a playbook.
35. Choose technology from an organizational perspective.

RULE 14

Macromanage

LET PEOPLE DO THEIR JOBS.

"The most pathetic person in the world is someone who has sight but no vision."

—Helen Keller

IN 2017, NATIONAL PUBLIC RADIO ran a remarkable news story about the organizational costs of micromanagement. The main takeaways of this piece were: a) Micromanagement was the single most common complaint people had about their bosses, and b) it extracted a heavy toll on employees and damaged internal company relationships.

The response from listeners was overwhelming. This story generated hundreds of impassioned posts to NPR's social media pages. Many of these posts shared firsthand examples of micromanagement as experienced by employees, some of which boggle the mind.

One office worker described a manager who purchased and installed software that tracked exactly what the employee was doing on the computer throughout the day. Another shared an unexpected critique from the boss, who happened to be passing near her cubicle: "I did not hear the lid of that highlighter click when you put it back on." Someone else mentioned a manager who limited the number of permissible trips to the bathroom. The employee was forced to bring a laptop into the facilities with them. (This gives a whole new meaning to the term "taking care of business.")

If you're still wondering what actual micromanagement is, those extreme examples should help dispel any lingering mystery. I share them with you for a couple of reasons. First, real micromanagement needs to be distinguished from good-faith process development, which we discussed in Rule 13. By now I hope the difference is obvious. Process development supports people. Micromanagement alienates and intimidates them and is, at its base, all about power. One of the powerful conclusions NPR drew in its follow-up on the initial story was that micromanagement is a form of workplace bullying, a point that seems hard to dispute when you consider the examples.

The other reason I mention these stories is to highlight a

practical point that should concern every sales leader. Hundreds of people responded so strongly, and so emotionally, to the original NPR story that they were compelled to go online right away and publicly share their own negative experiences with micromanagement—with their real names visible. That kind of instant, visceral response should tell you something: Micromanagement is a serious, widespread workplace problem—an issue that lots of employees recognize instantly from direct personal experience and don't want to see repeated in their lives. It is, in other words, a big deal. It is something to constantly be aware of.

The global pandemic of 2020 only made this situation worse for many sales teams, in my view. Companies having to change the way they did business caused many managers accustomed to doing their jobs in person to come to terms with a new working environment, one in which more and more salespeople made their contributions off-site. Some managers responded to the situation in exactly the wrong way—by increasing micromanagement instead of trusting their teams. In a post-pandemic workplace, this problem of micromanagement may be more serious than ever.

People working from home may experience this problem in particularly challenging ways. Many sales teams don't have adequate playbooks or processes in place for telecommuters to follow. At one end of the extreme, they may not get enough support. They may be told to "just get the job done" and be left to figure everything out for themselves. At the other extreme is micromanagement. The manager feels the job won't or can't get done without direct, in-person supervision, so they intervene constantly when they find themselves feeling pressure. This second scenario is one of the big reasons micromanagement is so expensive in terms of lost productivity, lost revenue, and lost talent.

That final problem, lost talent, is perhaps the most concerning. People who have to deal with experiences like the ones I shared at the beginning of this chapter usually end up leaving, often with major consequences for the companies in question. That's certainly not what you want.

A survey conducted by Trinity Solutions reported that 79% of respondents had personally experienced micromanagement, and that 69% actively considered changing positions as a result of interactions with supervisors who micromanaged.[15]

So here's a big question: Why do you hire salespeople? I hope it's because you believe they are talented and that they can help the company obtain the goals it has set. When you micromanage, though, you are saying you don't really believe any of that.

You are saying you have an issue with the salesperson, either because you have no faith that the job will be done correctly if you are not involved or you believe that nobody could possibly do the job better than you could. Neither of these beliefs hold up under logical scrutiny. Neither supports the aim of creating and supporting a self-correcting team, the kind of team that can scale its success as it grows.

Maybe you once had a boss who micromanaged you. Was that a pleasant experience? Did it make you a better problem-solver? Did it make you want to stick around? Also, be aware that the kind of supervision you got from your early bosses may not be what your employees need from you today. You may tell yourself that you are "training," but if the training never stops, regardless of how well the person does the job, then there is a problem you need to look at.

Micromanagement is a macro challenge. It is not where you want to be as a sales leader. In fact, it's the exact opposite of leadership. As a leader, you instead want to make macromanagement—leadership that steps back, understands the ultimate goal, empowers people, and unleashes both creativity and collaboration—the daily norm for your team. Here are some ideas on how to do that.

SALES LEADERSHIP KEY 36: CHECK THE MIRROR.

One of the biggest challenges about micromanagement is that it always comes camouflaged by good intentions. Often, sales leaders do not even realize they are doing it. If they did, they probably wouldn't micromanage. But it's time to face the facts. If a leader is not intentional about avoiding it, they're often doing it unconsciously.

There are lots of different ways a leader can go into denial about this. They may say that they are focusing on the customer experience, that they are catching damaging errors before they derail a presentation, or that they are pulling out the magnifying glass and identifying major obstacles to a salesperson's productivity that would otherwise go undetected. Here is the problem: If you have to do all that personally, all or most of the time, then you're not really being a leader. This makes you an operator. You are diminishing, not expanding, your influence. You have to find a way to be brutally honest with yourself about whether or not this is happening. You have to self-assess.

Here is a powerful question we ask leaders in our training: If you are making a habit of intervening in the daily operational work of one of your direct reports, why are you doing so?

It may be worth taking some time to consider this question closely as it relates to your sales team and your world. What we typically find in talking to leaders is that, while there are a lot of variations, there are really only three basic answers to this question.

1. **You don't have confidence in this salesperson's ability to fulfill the job requirements.** If this is the real-world situation you face, you must determine whether this is "skill" issue or a "will" issue. The salesperson must be both willing and able. If they lack the skills necessary to do the job but would be able to do the job with proper training and coaching, then your responsibility is to make sure the employee gets that training and coaching. If it's a "will" issue, the person can do the job but is simply not motivated to do so. In that case you have two options: reassign them to a role where they will be motivated to make a contribution or part company. Notice that doing the person's job is not an option here for the leader—unless for some reason it has to happen on a temporary basis while you find a replacement. (That should be a very rare outcome, of course, and you are far better off finding someone else to fill in than doing the work yourself.)
2. **The salesperson is a new hire and hasn't yet gotten up to speed on all the things it takes to succeed.** This may mean it makes sense to intervene from time to time and to build

in what you learn from the intervention as focused, carefully designed questioning during the coaching process. This way you can help the person take on personal ownership of the mission of getting up to speed. But it may also mean your onboarding process needs revamping, so that the new hire has access to all the tools and resources necessary to do the job and knows what the key best practices, the key benchmarks, and the key deadlines are during the critical 90-day ramp-up following the hire. There needs to be a clear behavioral plan, so that both you and the salesperson know what behaviors are needed for them to succeed. The goal is always to be phasing out your intervention in the employee's daily activities. Remember: The best-case scenario is that you don't have to intervene at all.

If neither of those situations describes the *why* behind your decision to intervene in your direct report's activities on a regular basis, the process of elimination leads to a painful, but necessary truth, one that it is vitally important for you to acknowledge if you want to grow and learn as a leader.

3. **You are micromanaging.** Something about the way this salesperson does the job makes it hard for you not to play the superhero, swing into action, and win some kind of credit for: a) averting certain disaster, b) "showing

'em how it's done," or c) doing both a) and b). If this is your situation, then the time has come for some straight talking from us to you: This is toxic behavior and it needs to change, fast.

Other people may have radically different working styles than you do. That's OK. Set the guardrails, set the objectives, step back, and let them do their job. If you continue to make a habit of micromanaging, you will lose good people, limit or eradicate your own influence, and slow the growth of your team. You will be unable to scale sales growth, and you will hurt your own career and certainly limit your rise in the company.

Hard truths are the most important ones to process, and this one is one of the hardest. Take some time to process it, and then move on to Sales Leadership Key 37, below.

SALES LEADERSHIP KEY 37: FOCUS ON THE FUTURE.

As a sales leader, you want to be working *on* the team as opposed to *in* the team. One of the biggest challenges of micromanaging is that it keeps you from doing this. Recognizing this challenge and responding to it constructively can be a truly liberating personal experience.

You cannot be the sales team's chief doer. There's only so much that you can do. There are only so many hours in the day.

The more you can remain up at 30,000 feet, piloting the plane to its destination, the better off you and your team are going to be.

That doesn't mean you don't have the option to go down to 5,000 feet when circumstances demand. Of course you do. But most of the time—the vast majority of the time—your job is to focus on and create the future. Once you've given a task to someone on your team, once you've set the benchmarks along with the check-in points and the contingency plans, you really do need to step back and let them do what you are paying them to do.

This may take some practice. It may take some coaching. It may take some trial and error. Remind yourself that all strong leaders have had to learn to let their team members operate on their own until one-on-one check-in time rolls around, even if they know the job is being done differently than they would do it.

It's discouraging to a person to give them a task and then ask them constantly how it's coming along, second-guess their decisions and methods, and otherwise find ways to treat them like grade schoolers. If you trusted them enough to hire them, trust them enough to get out of their way. Focus your attention on where you want the team to go next and how you're going to get there.

SALES LEADERSHIP KEYS: RULE 14

36. Check the mirror.

37. Focus on the future.

RULE 15

Become a Learning Team

COMMIT TO PERSONAL AND PROFESSIONAL DEVELOPMENT.

"Leadership and learning are indispensable to each other."

—John F. Kennedy

ASK A HUNDRED SALES LEADERS whether they support a learning culture, and you will likely get a hundred affirmative answers. Ask a hundred frontline salespeople who report directly or indirectly to those leaders whether they work in an organization that actually supports a learning culture, and you will see that number drop dramatically.

So how can sales leaders close the gap? If you want a learning-focused team and those who work for you don't experience that, what can you do?

Start by acknowledging that telling your team you want a learning culture does not mean that you will instantly have a learning culture. You have to go further. Your words must be paired with action. Here, then, are five Sales Leadership Keys you can use to ensure a high success rate when it comes to launching and following through on a commitment to a strong learning culture.

According to a ClearCompany study, 68% of respondents said training and development was the most important policy of the company they worked for.[16]

SALES LEADERSHIP KEY 38: CHANGE THE THINKING AT THE TOP.

Everything starts with how you think about your people. Sales leaders who are serious about initiating and supporting a learning culture stop treating the professional and personal development of the team as an expense and start treating it as what it really is: an investment.

Think about it. If you consistently invest in a learning culture, you are going to have a superior team. That means you will have a major edge in the marketplace. Your salespeople will be sharper, they will be better at connecting dots that the competition doesn't even notice, and they will be more adept at identifying and delivering value to the customer. Why wouldn't you make that investment?

Here's an interesting exercise. Do a quick inventory. Out of the last 90 days, how many were devoted to you learning something new or getting better at something? If you're feeling really brave, answer these as well: What about your team? Are there training and ongoing personal development paths created for each salesperson? How much time is spent learning? Or is all the learning "as needed"—which normally means it's reactive and never enough?

SALES LEADERSHIP KEY 39: KEEP AN EYE ON THE METRICS.

In particular, notice in which direction your retention numbers are moving. If more of your best and brightest people are leaving this month than last month, rest assured that the needle is moving in the wrong direction. On the other hand, if more of them are sticking around, then the needle is moving in the right direction. Ultimately, there are only two reasons why good salespeople who aren't dealing with a major life change will decide to leave your team: either they don't respect their manager, or they feel like they're not learning new things and growing. Creating a true learning culture for everyone on the team (including you) can turn around both of those unfortunate situations—and reduce your turnover numbers.

You can also identify creative ways to measure other critical metrics. For instance, how many of your team members share success stories demonstrating that they have put something they learned into practice? How many have shared important best practices with other salespeople? What kinds of contests can you set up that reward implementation of tactics your people have been taught? (For instance: Who can come up with, and deliver, the best "thirty-second commercial" for one of your products/ services?) How will you track the results of those contests?

SALES LEADERSHIP KEY 40: BUILD YOUR BENCH.

A great sports team doesn't just have a superior starting lineup; it has a superior collection of rising talent and a deep roster of utility players. They call that "bench strength"—and great companies have it, as well. With a strong learning culture, you have the ability to build up your bench, not just by making people stronger at their current positions and helping them make more and varied contributions but also by helping them begin to grow into the right future position before they take it on. Many sales managers have zero management experience when they're promoted. That's not how it should be.

To continue the sports metaphor: Would you ask someone who has never pitched a single inning to start in a trophy-determining playoff game? Probably not. A learning culture that features appropriate training, mentorship, and project experience can ensure that won't happen in your world. The value and the revenue that can be generated from your development plan is incredible. Make the most of it. Remember: Your job is to help make people as successful as possible in their current job—and get them ready for their next job. That means you must understand the ideal behaviors, attitudes, and techniques for each role and make sure people receive the appropriate coaching and training. (It also means you must be personally secure enough to encourage and support someone who wants to find a way to grow their way into the kind of job you now hold.)

Would you rather coach and train your salespeople knowing that they may leave, or not coach and train them and have them stick around? Think about it!

SALES LEADERSHIP KEY 41: CREATE PERSONALIZED LEARNING PATHS.

Once you know what someone needs to do to be successful in their current position, once you know what they will need to do to move into the next position that makes sense for them and for the organization, create a learning path that is unique to that individual. Never stop asking:

> "What experiences should this person have, and what results do they need to generate, in order to be successful at a particular job?"

"What tactics do they need to master to create those results?"

"What mindset should they have—meaning what habitual ways of looking at issues are likeliest to lead to success?"

"What behavioral plan should they be following so that they stay ahead of the curve, and so that nothing falls through the cracks?"

"How will I assess the team member against the most important benchmarks? How can I train and coach the person to close the gaps?"

Be careful. Learning paths cannot be team-wide or company-wide. They are job-specific and employee-specific. What Salesperson A needs to learn next is probably not going to be what Salesperson B needs to learn next. Always assess what makes a given team member different from everyone else on the team.

Note, too, that it's vitally important that salespeople co-create their learning plan. Let them participate. Instead of telling people what they should or could be getting from their development path, help them discover it for themselves through the questions you ask when you're meeting one-on-one. That way the learning path they commit to will have more potency and what they eventually learn will be far more likely to "stick." Learning will be an important personal priority for them—not just another edict coming from the boss.

SALES LEADERSHIP KEY 42: START THE LEARNING AT THE TOP.

At organizations with a strong learning culture, the leadership is always personally congruent with the culture. This means showing your leadership team, through both decisions and actions, that you are personally committed to learning and development—yours and theirs. So for instance, when you read a book that has the potential to have a positive impact, pass it along and, once everyone has read it, discuss it with your team. When you send people to outside training, ask them to share what they've learned with the rest of the team. Never forget that employees emulate the actions of senior leadership and tend to take on the same priorities as the leadership team. When you make learning part of your personal leadership style, it becomes an essential part of supporting a learning culture throughout your organization.

Teams, much like people, need to be continually moving forward. By setting and pursuing your own learning and development path, you'll be doing more than setting the right example for your salespeople. You'll also be backing up your good intentions by initiating and supporting a learning culture that rewards everyone for stretching beyond their comfort zone—starting with you.

SALES LEADERSHIP KEYS: RULE 15

38. Change the thinking at the top.
39. Keep an eye on the metrics.
40. Build your bench.
41. Create personalized learning paths.
42. Start the learning at the top.

RULE 16

Be Ready for Anything

PLAN, PREPARE, AND THEN BE FLEXIBLE.

"Houston, we have a problem."

—Jim Lovell

THE ULTIMATE TEST as a leader comes when you find a way to respond effectively to something you could not possibly have expected or anticipated. Situations like that—that you never could have seen coming—often have major implications for your team, for your organization, for your customers, and even for those who love you. If you plan to lead a team that can scale its sales growth, you must be prepared to deal with these issues constructively. That requires bringing a special skill to the table: the ability to re-evaluate and set up a whole new plan on the fly and then keep re-evaluating and adjusting as circumstances dictate.

Perhaps you've seen the film *Apollo 13*, based on the amazing true story of a 1970 space flight that changes from being a mission to the Moon to being a mission to survive when the spacecraft is crippled by an explosion. Life shifts into a radically different gear for the three-man crew and their support team back on Earth. They had prepared for one kind of mission, but the mission they faced was very different.

Fulfilling that kind of mission shift requires the ability to assess an entirely new set of challenges, the willingness to start planning from scratch without a lot of information, deep reservoirs of creativity and flexibility, and, last but certainly not least, the courage to go way, way beyond your personal comfort zone. Fortunately, the real-life story of Apollo 13 had a happy ending. As a sales leader, you may face challenges that make the same basic demands on you, and you must be ready to respond effectively.

In my book *The Road to Excellence*, I wrote about what I called the "leadership blind spots"—the critical challenges that leaders are all too often unaware of and unprepared for when positioning their organizations for long-term growth. Then 2020 happened, and everyone knows know what kinds of challenges came in its wake. During an interview in the spring of that extraordinary year, a reporter asked me, "As you were putting together your list of blind spots, did you ever consider that a global pandemic might need to be one of the entries in your book?"

As a matter of fact, I hadn't included something like a global pandemic when I put together that list. I did leave a blind spot off—an important one. It wasn't a global health emergency; it was that many leaders aren't psychologically ready to pivot as quickly as they can. For the pandemic, it took too long for many businesses to respond intelligently to changes that the environment forced upon them. For example, some restaurants switched overnight to takeout only, while others shut their doors and waited until they could reopen. You can guess which ones made it through more successfully. The same, of course, goes for sales teams. Some adapted better than others.

Learn from that experience. Be prepared to make big changes quickly, when the data and the circumstances say you should. That is the blind spot a lot of leaders missed. Many were caught off guard by this big reality check.

In 2020, the big reality check was a global health crisis, but it could have been anything—even a good, old-fashioned market correction. Who knows what it will be next time around?

Should what happened in 2020 really have taken everyone by surprise as completely as it did? Before you answer, consider that business leaders already know that every 10 years or so there's going to be a major market adjustment that will affect their business model. You have to expect that, at some point, you and your team will be called upon to turn on a dime. That must not spook you or cause you to freeze up. Consider an occasional reality check to be unavoidable, because history proves that it is.

Will you always be psychologically ready for these reality checks? Maybe not. Can you work to be prepared for the next one? I believe you can.

Imagining that there will never be another big reality check is, in my view, the true global blind spot for all leaders. There will always be another big, unexpected change to deal with. You can count on that. The only issue is whether you will respond quickly and effectively, like the Apollo 13 astronauts and the ground crew who were committed to the success of their evolving mission.

No matter how much you prepare, there will always be something that throws you a "Houston, we have a problem" moment. If you expect that moment, then it won't feel like a loss or a failure when it happens. You'll be able to take note of what happened and look for ways to update your own and your sales team's playbooks so you can be better prepared if it happens again.

When a reality check shows up in your business, there's no point moping, whining, or pointing fingers. Don't waste any time with the blame game. There will be plenty of time for in-depth investigations later. In the moment, when it's upon you, focus on constructive action. Assess the issue, come up with solutions, and implement them. The less time your team and your business spends offline or operating at diminished capacity as the result of a business crisis, the better off everyone in the organization will be.

That's the big takeaway. Here are three more ideas that will help you prepare for and thrive in the face of any new reality check that may come your way.

According to Datto, a major downtime incident can end up costing a company anywhere from $10,000 per hour for smaller businesses to over $5 million per hour for enterprises.[17]

SALES LEADERSHIP KEY 43: SUPPORT THE EMERGING SALES LEADERS.

Of course, you will need to give revenue generation a high priority in a company crisis. That means you want to double down on supporting both sales and emerging sales management talent.

The best current estimates are that 43% of sales managers do not receive effective training prior to taking up the role. As if that weren't enough, some 32% of sales managers report that the ongoing training they do receive is less than effective.* That is unacceptable in normal times, but it is strategically dangerous during an emergency. Give the members of your team the support they deserve by providing all the training, all the tools, all the coaching, and all the personally customized support they need. The sales team is the revenue generator of your organization. Make sure that everyone on that team is ready to do the job and is fully equipped.

Today, there is a lot of money and a lot of attention being spent on sales enablement—that is, technology that gets sales forces ready to be successful. My opinion is that companies should focus on sales manager enablement first, because otherwise sales enablement is a wasted investment.

SALES LEADERSHIP KEY 44: BE OPEN TO INNOVATION.

Innovation is a matter of organizational mindset and corporate culture. Phrases like, "We have never done that," "It won't work," "It didn't work last time we tried it," and "Why not spend time on more important things?" all need to be thrown out the window, especially in a crisis. Start connecting unrelated dots and creating new perspectives. Look for alliances that you might never have considered in the past. For instance, business agreements

* Source: Sandler Research Center.

with people you once regarded as enemies or competitors may make perfect sense in a crisis. You may do things slightly differently from each other, but, collectively, you will have a better service offering. That's just one example—you get the idea. Be open to new thinking. Run innovation clinics within your sales team to bubble up all the good ideas, using the Team Storm process I've shared with you. Remember that innovative ideas can come from anywhere, not just from you. You have great people working with you—let them be innovators.

Innovation also means being willing and able to adjust your plan for the team. When a dramatically new set of circumstances emerges, you will likely need to set up a new six-month to one-year plan, based on the real-world situation you now face. Don't make the mistake of marching in lockstep to fulfill a plan that is no longer relevant to the world in which you and your people live.

SALES LEADERSHIP KEY 45: SET CLEAR EXPECTATIONS.

In order to ensure the machine is running smoothly and everyone on the team is self-sufficient, even during challenging times, make sure your expectations are crystal clear. This is you, the sales leader, driving the specific initiatives necessary to implement your team's six-month to one-year plan, which, as I say, may have been totally redesigned by now, based on what's currently going on in your world.

When there's an emergency, make sure that you are communicating with total clarity about those initiatives and about the specific deliverables that connect to them. Creating clear expectations takes away the ambiguity and uneasiness people may feel about trying to figure out what to do next. It also removes the anxiety and frustration you may feel about results that don't match what you wanted. People come to you with their own views and opinions, and they can very easily go down a path they believe is correct but is not what you wanted. This is why you have to be sure to set the right expectations up front. Setting expectations is the most important thing a salesperson can do on a sales call—it's also the most important thing to do as a leader of the sales team. Here's the checklist:

1. Explain what you want and why you want it. Be specific.
2. Set dates for when you want it; make sure the salesperson agrees that what you want is doable. It's fine if the dates you have in mind are a bit of a stretch—just make sure they are not perceived as unrealistic.
3. Explain exactly what success looks like.

4. Create benchmarks so you can measure success and adjust if necessary along the way.
5. Have the employee validate what they heard and what's expected by repeating it back to you.
6. Then, ask what you as the leader can do to support them—and listen carefully to what comes back.

Yes, some reality checks may catch people by surprise. Some cause chaos and disorientation that few could have imagined or anticipated. But, believe it or not, the reality checks you experience can also grant an unexpected favor—exposing your biggest blind spot of being unprepared to make effective adjustments. If you take the steps shared in this chapter, you can go a long way to fixing that blind spot once and for all. You can prepare your team to respond more effectively to challenges and to thrive in the new environment waiting for you when the next big reality check comes along.

SALES LEADERSHIP KEYS: RULE 16

43. Support the sales leaders.
44. Be open to innovation.
45. Set clear expectations.

EPILOGUE

I BELIEVE THAT it's crucial to never stop trying to become a better leader. No one is ever really finished with the task of learning what great leadership is. There are always new circumstances that show there is more to learn, more to experience, more to share. It is possible that someday another sixteen rules will emerge as being just as vital as those I've shared with you in these pages. Even so, these rules I have shared are indispensable starting points for teams that aim to position themselves to scale their sales growth. Through the years as company president and CEO, I have tried to improve the Sandler Training® methodology in accordance with them.

I will share one final thought from my mentor before I close, an insight that is as relevant today as it was when he first shared it with me decades ago. From David Sandler: "You can be part of your plan or a part of someone else's."

That's the advice I leave you with: Set your own plan. Use what you have learned here to put that plan into practice and make it a reality. If you want some support along the way, we are here for you. Visit us at sandler.com.

ENDNOTES

Introduction (page xvi)

[1]University of Warwick study: "Happiness and Productivity," Andrew J. Oswald, Eugenio Proto, and Daniel Sgroi (March, 2014) warwick.ac.uk/newsandevents/pressreleases/new_study_shows/

Rule 1 (page 8)

[2]Trust Across America's FACTS Framework (2018) www.trustacrossamerica.com/documents/index/Return-Methodology.pdf

Rule 2 (page 12)

[3]*Harvard Business Review*, "How to Manage a Toxic Employee," Amy Gallo (October 3, 2016) hbr.org/2016/10/how-to-manage-a-toxic-employee

Rule 3 (page 36)

[4]Gallup, "State of the American Workplace Report" (2017) www.gallup.com/workplace/238085/state-american-workplace-report-2017.aspx

Rule 4 (page 50)

[5]*Forbes* magazine, "How Does Coaching Actually Help Leaders?" Carly Sime (March 28, 2019) www.forbes.com/sites/carleysime/2019/03/28/how-does-coaching-actually-help-leaders/

Rule 5 (page 60)

[6]*Contemporary Educational Psychology,* "Writing about Personal Goals and Plans Regardless of Goal Type Boosts Academic Performance," Michaéla C. Schippers, Dominique Morisano, Edwin A. Locke, W.A. Scheepers, Gary P. Latham, Elisabeth M. de Jong (January, 2020) www.sciencedirect.com/science/article/pii/S0361476X1930428X

Rule 6 (page 72)

[7]Extended DISC validation study (2015) Extendeddisc.org

Rule 7 (page 82)

[8]*Policy Insights from the Behavioral and Brain Sciences,* Vol. 5, "How We Remember Conversation: Implications in Legal Settings," Sarah Brown-Schmidt, Aaron S. Benjamin (2018) labs.psychology.illinois.edu/~asbenjam/pubs/Brown-Schmidt%20&%20Benjamin,%202018.pdf

Rule 8 (page 91)

[9]*Journal of Personality and Social Psychology,* "The Power Motive as an Influence on Group Decision Making," E.M. Fodor and T. Smith, 1982. doi.apa.org/doiLanding?doi=10.1037%2F0022-3514.42.1.178

Rule 9 (page 104)

[10]PSA Financial Services article, "Most Fortune 500 Companies Have Mentor Programs. Do You?" Tara Bolotin (March, 2019) www.psafinancial.com/2018/03/most-fortune-500-companies-have-mentor-programs-do-you/

Rule 10 (page 108)

[11]Landmark Workplace Accountability Study, quoted in *Forbes* magazine, "The Five Rules Followed by Accountable Leaders," Paloma Cantero-Gomez, (June, 2019) www.forbes.com/sites/palomacanterogomez/2019/06/07/the-5-rules-followed-by-accountable-leaders/

Rule 11 (page 120)

[12]Troop Messenger article, "Five Essential Statistics on the Power of Collaboration," Vyshnavi Basuthkar (August, 2019) www.troopmessenger.com/blogs/workplace-collaboration-statistics

Rule 12 (page 133)

[13]Dominican University in California study led by Gail Mathews, quoted in *Inc.* magazine, "This Is the Way You Need to Write Down Your Goals for Faster Success," Peter Economy (February, 2018) www.inc.com/peter-economy/this-is-way-you-need-to-write-down-your-goals-for-faster-success.html

Rule 13 (page 144)

[14]AI Multiple article, "55 Process Improvement Case Studies and Project Results" (January 2021) research.aimultiple.com/process-improvement-case-studies/

Rule 14 (page 150)

[15]Trinity Solutions survey quoted in *PA Times*, "Damaging Effects of Micromanagment," Linda Barnes (March 2015) patimes.org/damaging-effects-micromanagement/

Rule 15 (page 160)

[16]Clear Company survey quoted in HR Exchange Network article, "Seven Stats that Prove Training Value," Mason Stevenson (August 2019) www.hrexchangenetwork.com/learning/news/7-stats-that-prove-training-value

Rule 16 (page 171)

[17]Datto article, "Discover the True Cost of Downtime," Chris Brunau (July 2018) www.datto.com/au/blog/the-cost-of-downtime